The Heart of Paul

A Relational Paraphrase of the
NEW TESTAMENT

Ben Campbell Johnson

VOLUME **1**

The Heart of Paul

A Relational Paraphrase of the
NEW TESTAMENT

Ben Campbell Johnson

VOLUME
1

Word Books, Publisher
Waco, Texas

THE HEART OF PAUL

Printed in the United States of America

ISBN 0–87680–475–X

Library of Congress catalog card number: 76–19531

Contents

Introduction

I hope you will take time to read these brief introductory remarks. I make such a bold request of you because I assume introductions are infrequently read.

I invite you to look inside my mind and to discover my intention in paraphrasing *The Heart of Paul.* I suppose in the purest definition of the word this is not a "paraphrase" because, by its nature, it lies somewhere between a careful paraphrase and a one-line commentary. You will find that my effort is more interpretative than exacting. In this sense, every generation must paraphrase the gospel.

By "relational paraphrase" I am confessing that my approach to truth is relational, i.e., that I do not know truth as objective outside myself nor totally subjective within myself. Truth lies in relationships . . . so, the truth about God, for example, is discovered and expressed through our relationship to him.

In my endeavor to hear God speak his word in my situation, I have read Paul's letters to the Christians of his day and asked, "What is Paul endeavoring to say to these Christians about God, Jesus Christ, the Holy Spirit, the Church, man, and the Christian lifestyle?" As the answers to this questioning have crystallized in my mind, I have tried to express those meanings

[7

in words and phrases which are helpful to me in my Christian living. I share the result of my discoveries in this paraphrase with the hope that it may shed light upon your own journey.

I confess to you at the outset that I am not writing as a scholar. However, I am not devoid of academic qualifications, having seventy-two accredited hours in New Testament Greek, a Master of Theology degree in New Testament, and further graduate studies in philosophy and religion. I do not come to the Scriptures as a novice. As a young Christian, I memorized the greater part of these letters from the Authorized Version.

I have several basic assumptions which will be evidenced as you read this paraphrase. I believe that God created the world for his purpose which is good; that he made human beings in his own image to reflect and participate in his purpose. In Jesus Christ, God has declared that every person has a new relationship with him. Both in the original creation and in the new creation in Jesus Christ, God purposes the fulfillment of every person, the fulfillment of creation, and the fulfillment of his own person. This is a basis for a "Theology of Fulfillment." You will be aware of this perspective in my paraphrase of the word *glory* which to me suggests fulfillment.

I would like to suggest to you a relational pattern of Bible study which has proved helpful to me. It consists of four phases. Begin by selecting any section of Scripture and numbering the paragraphs.

Phase 1. Underline the words and phrases which are significant to you.

Phase 2. Read the first paragraph and ask, "What question must have been asked for Paul to write this paragraph?"

Phase 3. Read each paragraph carefully with two questions in mind: "What is God saying to me today through this paragraph?" and, "What decision will I make because God has so addressed me?"

Phase 4. Summarize what Paul teaches in each section under these headings: God, Jesus Christ, the Holy Spirit, the Church, Christian Experience, the Christian Lifestyle, the Future.

You can use this format for individual research for a relational understanding of Paul. I believe your experience of this study will be greatly enhanced by a small group in which you can share with others your insights and receive their understanding.

I cannot close this introduction without a word of appreciation to my very able editor, Harriette Griffin; to a friend, Arthur Wainwright, who has offered me many valuable suggestions; and to my wife, Nan, who permitted me the solitude of many early morning hours to write this paraphrase.

My appreciation also must go to Floyd Thatcher of Word Inc., for his encouragement in the completion of this task.

BEN JOHNSON

Romans

INTRODUCTION

Of all Paul's books in the New Testament, his letter to the church at Rome is probably his heaviest and most influential piece of writing. In style, it is more a treatise than the personal, intimate kind of correspondence he wrote to the Galatians or the Corinthians, for example. In terms of content it does not deal with the particular problems of a particular church, as others of Paul's letters do, but instead is an extended statement of his understanding of the Christian faith.

Paul did not found the church in Rome (historians are unsure who did), nor had he ever visited there. His reasons for writing the letter to the Romans were, first, to introduce himself to them in advance of his anticipated visit, and, second and more important, to present a carefully thought out, inclusive exposition of the faith. Paul wrote the letter from Corinth around A.D. 57.

The bulk of the letter is divided into two main parts—1:16–11:36 and 12:1–15:33.

The first section is Paul's commentary on the Christian gospel, the gist of which may be found in 1:16–17—"I am confident that the good news will release God's dynamic energy which makes all persons whole. Through this communication God's true nature and activity are shown *to* those who trust him *through* those who trust him. Long ago it was written, 'The whole person lives through trust.' "

The second part is the so-called practical section in which

[11

Paul turns from the theoretical to the functional. In other words, if you "permit the Spirit of God within to transform your being and behavior," (12:2), what does that look like in practical, everyday terms?

Chapter 16 is something of a puzzle because it does not seem to be directly related to the rest of the book. If Paul had never visited Rome, how could he possibly know so many people in that church? Most scholars believe that chapter 16 came from a separate Pauline letter and somehow got attached to Romans over the years. Another interesting theory is that Paul decided to send a copy of his Romans letter to Ephesus, and thus added the last chapter of personal messages to the members of that church.

ROMANS

1 [1] I am Paul, a loyal follower of Jesus Christ. I have been given a special commission to speak God's good news, so I center my life around it. [2] God pledged this good news a long time ago through messengers who recorded his pledge in our records.

[3-4] God later announced this good news through his Son, Jesus Christ our Lord, who was physically descended from King David and spiritually quite convincingly has been declared "Son of God" by rising from death.

[5-6] Through this Son of God I have received unconditional love and my special commission to announce to all nations that they are called to belong to God, and my responsibility includes you who have accepted Jesus Christ. [7] As special messenger I, Paul, am writing to all of you at Rome, you who are called to be Godpersons, inviting you into a whole life. May unconditional love and peace be yours through God our Father and the Lord Jesus Christ.

Paul's feelings about the good news

[8] First of all, I thank God that your faith is recognized and acclaimed everywhere.

[9] I respond to God with my whole being because of the good news his Son has brought. He knows that I constantly pray for you, [10] and always request him to give me an itinerary that will include you. [11] I am eager to see you because I want to awaken a gift of the Spirit within you which will enable you to mature. [12] And for myself, I need your encouragement and recognition through the trust we both have.

[13] I do want you to recognize that frequently I have made plans to visit you so that I could reproduce my life in you as I

have in other non-Jews. So far, though, I have been unable to get these plans to materialize. [14] I feel indebted to cultured and uncultured alike, to wise and foolish, [15] and therefore with all the energy I have left I want to proclaim the good news to you in Rome. [16] I am confident that the good news will release God's dynamic energy which makes all persons whole. [17] Through this communication God's true nature and activity are shown *to* those who trust him *through* those who trust him. Long ago it was written, "The whole person lives through trust."

Those who live outside God's intention

[18] God has already shown his attitude toward those persons who live contrary to his purpose and intention, who have been exposed to reality but continue to contradict it with their choices and actions. [19] They have been exposed to that which can be recognized about God because it is evident in their own natures. God has shown it to them within themselves. [20] God's essential nature, his eternal authority and his deity, though veiled to direct human inspection, has been glimpsed and grasped from the beginning of creation in the works he created. So now they have no excuse for living as if God did not exist.

[21] They have no excuse because they had an awareness of God through his creation, and yet they did not reverence God nor properly appreciate their own worth. Rather, their imagination with its undisciplined impulses led them to more and more emptiness, and their surrender to their undisciplined drives caused them to lose touch with their true selves. [22] They claimed superintelligence, but actually were quite foolish. [23] They even made the ultimate fulfillment of the imperishable God into a perishable idol shaped like perishable creatures.

[24] God permitted them to give full expression to their imaginative desires by abusing their bodies with each other. [25] They perverted the truth about God, making it fake, and their center of devotion and worship became the created world rather than

14]

the Creator, who deserves our highest priority. [26] When they made this deliberate choice, God permitted them to pervert all their natural desires into unnatural activities. [27] Both the women and the men engaged in a variety of homosexual activities which I feel embarrassed to describe, and they have experienced the frustration of their sexual fulfillment which this behavior produces.

[28] Because they had decided not to recognize God, he permitted them to fill their minds with empty images and foolish fantasies which produced a wide variety of unfulfilling behavior: [29] bad relationships, sexual experiments without commitment, irresponsibility, grasping for fulfillment through material things, destroying each other, resenting each other, killing each other, [30] undermining and cutting each other down, God-haters, users of others, self-sufficient, self-acclaimers, creators of evil, disrespectful of parents, [31] blind to reality, undependable, perverted in their affections, unforgiving. [32] These persons know God's attitude toward their behavior, yet they not only continue in it, but take pleasure in it. Indeed, they are on their way to death.

We are all subject to God's evaluation

2 [1] But you Jews have no right to condemn another person; when you condemn the behavior I have just described, you actually condemn yourself because in principle you practice the same deeds. [2] God is justified in rejecting your behavior because he has all the facts. [3] Do you think for one moment, my fellow Jew, that when you condemn the behavior of non-Jews, you will escape God's evaluation of you? [4] Perhaps you resent the depths of his good will and patience and tolerance with them. Don't you realize that his goodness inspires a changed life in you?

[5] Look at yourself. You are insensitive and unwilling to change, and you daily widen the contradiction between what you are and what God ultimately intends. [6] On the day of the

[15

fulfillment of all things, God will give to every person precisely what each one has created for himself or herself. [7] Those who persist in living in harmony with their true selves and who thereby search for fulfillment, integrity, and continuation will find ultimate fulfillment. [8] But those who resist their deepest impulses, who are unresponsive to their true identity and seek substitute fulfillments, will be left empty and confused. [9] Every person who does not fulfill his destiny as a human being will experience an indescribable loss and the consequent pain of it, whether he is a Jew or a non-Jew. [10] But every person who lives in accordance with his identity will find fulfillment, integrity, and the unity of his being. This applies both to the Jews who first had revealed truth and to the non-Jews who later received good news.

[11] You see, God does not play favorites. Those who have contradicted his intention without having his revealed rules will experience the consequence of their choices. [12] Those who have deliberately contradicted God's rules will be evaluated in light of their knowledge of them. [13] (Having the rules does not count; it is keeping them.)

[14] When the outsiders, the non-Jews, who do not have the rules, keep the intent of the rules naturally, they, in a sense, acquire their own rules. [15] This fact demonstrates that God's rules are written in their inner being, and something inside tells them when they are living in harmony with God and when they are not—they either feel whole or contradictory. [16] The ultimate reckoning will come when God evaluates every person through Jesus Christ in accordance with my interpretation of the good news.

The rules will not make you a special person to God

[17] Now let me anticipate your defense. You will begin by making your claim of being a Jew: you trust in the rules and in the fact that you have a special call from God. [18] You say, "We know God's will and we affirm the values set forth in the rules."

¹⁹ You are confident that you can direct the confused and enlighten the unenlightened. ²⁰ Since you have in your rules a form of knowledge and reality, you think you can instruct others in God's way and nurture them in his intention for their lives.

²¹ I must help you see the weakness in the case you have built. While you teach others, do you learn anything yourself? You preach against stealing, but don't you steal? ²² You say that adultery is wrong, but do you commit adultery? You say you hate idols, but do you have idols of your own? ²³ My point is that your entire case is based on the rules, and in breaking those rules you dishonor God whom you claim to affirm. ²⁴ Your life is such a poor example of your teaching that the non-Jews disregard God altogether. ²⁵ Don't you recall our teaching? Being born into our group and properly initiated is of value only if we keep all the rules; but if we break the rules, our rights by birth and our initiation are canceled. ²⁶ So if the non-Jew who is uninitiated keeps the intent of the rules, doesn't this performance count for the initiation itself? ²⁷ And, I will go a step further. The uninitiated non-Jew who fulfills the intent of the rules will evaluate those of you who have the rules but don't live in accord with them. ²⁸ I have become convinced that being a special person to God is not determined by externals; nor is the true initiation physical. ²⁹ Being special to God is an inward matter, and true initiation into God's family is in the heart. The true children of God are more concerned with his acceptance of them than they are with human acceptance or rejection.

3 ¹ You may justly ask, "What profit is there then in being a Jew? Or, how does the initiation improve our standing?" ² I answer, "Being a Jew is to your advantage in many ways, particularly because God entrusted you with his promises for the whole world." ³ It doesn't matter if some did not trust God's promises. Their unfaith cannot undermine the faithfulness of God. ⁴ Never! Let God be recognized as faithful even when every human is deceitful. Of God's faithfulness the records say, "When you speak, you will be vindicated and cleared when you are on trial."

⁵ You may continue your self-justifying argument by saying, "But if our unfaith shows more clearly the faithfulness of God, is not God unfair to punish us?" (Understand, I'm reasoning humanly.) ⁶ Certainly not! For if that were true, how could God judge the world? ⁷ To state the question another way: "If the reality of God is more clearly perceived by my misrepresentation of it, why am I labeled an offender? ⁸ Or, why don't we do evil so that it may result in good?"—a false charge that some are making of me. (To condemn these persons is certainly just.)

We are all estranged from God

⁹ What is our conclusion? Are we Jews better than the non-Jews? Not at all! That's the whole point I have established; both Jews and non-Jews are estranged from God. The records affirm it:

¹⁰ No one is truly in harmony with God's plan;
    not a one.
¹¹ No one really understands himself,
    nor really seeks for God.
¹² All have gotten off the track,
    spending energy in ways that do not fulfill them.
    No one performs well, not one.
¹³ From their throats spews the deadness of their lives;
    their tongues have spoken in contradiction to the way they
        live.
¹⁴ Poison is what comes from their lips;
    and their talk is all bitter profanity.
¹⁵ Their feet run to attack others,
¹⁶ and they are destructive in style and miserable in life—
¹⁷ they do not experience unity in their being,

18]

[18] nor do they reverence God.

[19] Here is the proof that God's rules apply to everyone who is subject to them—and that means everybody. In fact, no one can open his mouth in self-defense because the whole world is accountable to God. [20] I have concluded, therefore, that no one gets a right relationship with God by trying to keep the rules. The rules only make us aware of the boundaries and tell us how the game is to be played.

A right relationship with God comes through trust in Christ

[21] But now, a way to have a right relationship with God that has nothing to do with the rules has been shown to us. It has even been attested to by our own records (the law and the prophets, as we are accustomed to saying). [22] I am referring to a right relationship with God which is offered to everyone who will receive it through trusting Jesus Christ. [23] And everyone needs it because at this point there is no difference between us; all of us have gotten off the track of God's original intention and have missed the fulfillment for which we were destined. [24] And all of us who believe God have a right relationship with him through his unconditional love which he revealed in Jesus Christ. [25] When Christ offered himself on the cross, God was declaring that our failures and futile efforts to fulfill our lives are completely forgiven through his patience and love. [26] Through Jesus Christ, God shows his consistency in being faithful to himself and to us who believe in Jesus.

[27] Who can brag, then, about having a right relationship with God? Nobody! Why? Because it's not an achievement earned by keeping rules or doing good. [28] A right relationship with God is received by faith. So, you must see that each person receives this right relationship without keeping the rules.

[29] Is this free gift offered only to the Jews? No, it is offered equally to the non-Jews. [30] You see, God offers a relationship to

both the initiated and the uninitiated through faith. [31] You may ask, "Do we invalidate the rules through faith?" Not at all; rather, we set them in proper perspective.

Abraham is an example of trust

4 [1] Where does our ancestor Abraham's life fit into this "new way"? You see, if Abraham achieved a right relationship with God by his own efforts, he has something to brag about, though not before God. [2] If a person could achieve a right relationship with God, he would have a basis for pride —but it wouldn't be pride in what God has done. [3] What does the record say? "Abraham trusted God, and he was accepted into a right relationship with God." [4] A person who works to earn a relationship gets it as a debt paid, not as a gift given. [5] But those who don't try to earn a relationship but rather trust the one who accepts freely those estranged from him, their very trust is counted for a right relationship. [6] The psalmist David described the happiness of everyone who has a right relationship with God without trying to achieve it by keeping the rules: [7] "How happy are the persons whose breaches of the rules are forgiven, whose disobedience to God is overlooked! [8] How happy they are who don't have their misdeeds counted against them by God!"

[9] Is this happiness for the "initiated" only, or can the uninitiated be happy as well? We have agreed that Abraham's trust was accepted as a basis for a right relation with God, but [10] what was his situation when this happened—initiated or uninitiated? It happened when he was uninitiated. That is your answer. [11] And, he received his initiation as a sign and seal of his relationship through trust. He therefore became the ancestor of all who trust God's promise, even though they have not received the physical initiation to show they are related to God. [12] He is also the ancestor of the initiated who don't count on the rite of initiation but follow his example and

trust God's promise (as, I remind you, Abraham did before he was initiated).

God's pledge to Abraham was made because of faith

[13] God's pledge to make Abraham the heir of the world was not made to him or his offspring because he kept rules, but because of his trust relationship with God. [14] If Abraham's offspring who live by the rules receive the inheritance, trust is invalidated and the promise of God emptied of content. [15] The rules provide a basis for punishment, not a positive relationship. Where there are no rules, there can be no breaking them, with the consequent punishment. [16] Therefore, a right relationship is offered to the person who trusts God, so that it may be a gift which validates the promise to everyone, not only to the rulekeepers, but to the believers like Abraham, the ancestor of us all.

[17] Let me remind you of the kind of faith Abraham had. Recall the promise, "I have made you the ancestor of many nations." God, in whose presence Abraham lived, made him that promise. I repeat: God, who makes the dead come alive; God, who calls nonexisting things into being; this God made the promise to Abraham. [18] And Abraham, who had no grounds for hope, through hope trusted that he would populate the world, believing in the promise that his offspring would be as numerous as the stars in the sky and the sands on the shore. [19] He never wavered in his trust, and he refused to believe in his body's sterility or Sarah's barrenness. [20] He didn't permit lack of trust to stagger his confidence in God's promise, [21] but instead his trust made him strong and so brought fulfillment to God. He was confident that God, who gives life to the dead and calls creation into being, would fulfill the promise he had made. [22] Because he had this kind of trust, God received him into right relationship with himself.

[23] When the record says that Abraham's trust in God gave

[21

him a right relationship, it is not talking only about Abraham but also about us. [24] We too receive a relationship by trusting God who raised Jesus our Lord from death; [25] he died for us and our failures; he was raised to set our record clear with God.

Being in union with God through Christ

5 [1] Because we are now in right relationship with God through trusting his promise to accept us, we are united to him through Jesus Christ our Lord. [2] Christ has enabled us to receive this gift of God's unconditional love by which we are established in this new life. And because we live in this love, we celebrate life in anticipation of the ultimate fulfillment of God. [3] But not only that—we also celebrate our hardships. [4] Pain enables us to learn patience, patience enables us to be more aware of what we experience, and the more deeply we experience life, the greater hope we have. [5] And, our hope will not be disappointed because God's love fills our inner being through his Holy Spirit whom he has given us.

[6] It was at the very time that we were quite helpless in the face of alienation and death, that Christ gave himself for us who were unaware of God. [7] For a person to offer his life for a good person who is living in complete awareness of God would be rather unexpected; yet, perhaps, some would be willing to die for such a good person. [8] But God showed how much he loves us by having Christ die for us when we were both disobedient and helpless.

[9] If, then, we have a right relationship with God through Christ's death, it is even more true that we will be delivered from meaninglessness through his life. [10] If Christ through his death created a truce between us and God when we were acting like God's enemies, now that we are at peace won't he make us whole through his life? [11] So we are not only glad about the future, but at this very moment we are happy because God has made us one with himself through Jesus Christ.

From sin and death to unconditional love

[12] Here is how it works: Sin entered human experience through one man, and death is the consequence of sin; so, since all men die, all have participated in sin and its consequences. [13] Obviously, sin was in human experience before God gave the rules, but there can be no infraction of the rules until the rules are made. [14] Still, even the people born after Adam committed his sin and before Moses received his rules had to and did die, though their sin was not a repeat of Adam's (who, incidentally, foreshadowed the later appearance of Christ.)

[15] The single act of Adam and the single act of Christ are similar in that they affect everyone, but the effect is quite different. Through Adam many have died; but through the unconditional love of God and the communication of that love through Christ, many have come alive. [16] And, there is yet another contrast in the effect of these two acts. By one of them, all persons were judged guilty and condemned; by the other, all were given the free gift of acceptance and a new beginning. [17] Consider still another comparison. If by Adam's disobedience death ruled human existence, it is even more true that those who receive the overflow of God's unconditional love and the gift of a right relationship with him will rule their lives by Jesus Christ.

[18] Let me summarize my argument. By one person's disobedience judgment was passed on the human race and all were condemned; in the same way, by the rightness of one man the gift of God's love was given to all people, telling them they are okay. [19] Just as one man opened the door for all to experience estrangement from God, the other gave to all a right relationship with God. [20] The rules were given to make us more acutely aware of the misdirection of our lives, but no matter how great our misdirection and frustration, the unconditional love of God is always greater. [21] That means that where sin and death have obsessed human awareness and

[23

ruled existence in the past, now the unconditional love of God will rule through right relationships to the ultimate fulfillment of life through Jesus Christ our Lord.

The new life we have in Christ

6 [1] How shall we respond, then, to our new situation? Shall we continue to break rules and seek fulfillment through our old patterns of behavior so that God can keep on giving us his unconditional love? [2] Not at all. We have died to our old style of life, so how can we continue to practice it? [3] Please realize that when we were initiated into our relationship with Jesus Christ, we were initiated into his death. [4] Just as our bodies were pressed down into the water, our old lifestyle was submerged in the death of Christ; and just as Christ was lifted out of death to fulfill God's purpose, we can now fulfill his intention for us by living a whole new kind of life.

[5] Since we have participated in his death, we will also participate in the new life his resurrection releases. [6] We are aware that our old style of life died with him, and the urge to live apart from him has been stifled so that we are no longer controlled by old habits and attitudes. [7] You know that when a person dies physically, he is liberated from his estranged existence, [8] and since we have died (as it were) with Christ, we believe that we have also come alive through the new principle of life he revealed. [9] We know that Christ's resurrection means that he will not die again nor ever be subject to death in any way. [10] When he died, he renounced everything that estranges from God; in his life he is in perfect union with God.

[11] Just as Christ died and came to life, consider yourself dead to the life you lived when you were estranged from God but alive now to him and a new way of life through Jesus Christ our Lord. [12] Don't let your old habits and patterns of life control you today, even though you will have strong impulses to do so. [13] Don't get "hooked" into those old attitudes

and actions that are nonproductive and unfulfilling, but open yourself fully to God and permit him to inspire a new way of thinking, feeling, and behaving. [14] Then the old way of life will not control you because you are not living by rules but in the unconditional love of God.

A lifestyle that reflects a right relation with God

[15] Does this mean that we ought to give expression to every feeling and desire because we are living in the unconditional love of God and not according to rules? Of course not! [16] Surely you know that whatever controls you is your master. If you choose to surrender to the kind of life you lived when God didn't matter, that choice will mean death to you. If, on the other hand, you choose to respond to the impulses of God's love, the result will be a life in right relationship with God.

[17] Thank God that whereas you used to be enslaved by a lifestyle that does not recognize God, now in your inmost being you have responded to his offer of unconditional love. [18] Free now from your old state of being and way of life, you have chosen to serve God and live a new life. [19] I am going to speak very clearly to you because I don't want you to miss my message. You had previously given yourself to a style of life, as I wrote earlier, that I am ashamed to describe. Don't do that any more, but give yourselves just as passionately to God, who will enable you to discover the right way to live as well as personal wholeness.

[20] When you were enslaved in your previous lifestyle, you were lost in a maze of meaninglessness and didn't know which turn to take. [21] What did that style of life produce which gives you a sense of accomplishment today? I repeat: that way of life only causes you shame today and results in death. [22] But now, being liberated from your estrangement by living in union with God, you are experiencing wholeness of life and anticipating the ultimate fulfillment. [23] Let me say it once

[25

again. The pay-off for a life lived apart from God is death, but God's gift is eternal life through Jesus Christ our Lord.

How the rules work

7 ¹ My friends, you are acquainted with our national rules. You will recall that these rules are in effect as long as a person lives. ² For example, a woman is bound to her husband by the rules as long as he lives, but when her husband dies, she is released from that particular rule. ³ If she remarries while her husband is alive, according to the rules, she will be labeled an adulteress. If her husband dies, she is free from that rule and is not an adulteress even though she marries again. ⁴ I use this example to illustrate to you, my friends, that you are released from the rules by your participation in the body of Christ. You are free to be united to Christ in his resurrection, and in this relationship you can live a life which fulfills the purpose of God.

⁵ When we were trying to gain God's approval by our own efforts, our impulses toward evil, which were awakened by the rules, motivated behavior that results in death. ⁶ But now we are free from those rules; we are dead to the way of life in which we were imprisoned and can serve God in the new way of the Spirit, not in the old way of the written rules.

The rules in relation to sin

⁷ Do we conclude then that the rules are sinful? Not really. I wouldn't have recognized sin except for the rules. I wouldn't have recognized my insatiable desire for more and more things unless the rule had stated, "You must not covet." ⁸ My alienation from God, awakened by the rules, triggered in me every kind of perverted desire. Without the rules I was unaware of my alienation from God.

⁹ In a period of innocence I was alive but unaware of the rules. Then I heard the rules which awakened me to the con-

tradiction in my being, and I felt my estrangement. [10] The rules which were intended to bring wholeness brought estrangement [11] that blurred my vision of reality and threatened to wipe out my being. [12] But remember that the rules are for wholeness, and God's directives are intended to bring wholeness, right relationship, and a good life. [13] Can we really say that what God intended to bring life actually brought death to me? Not really. You see, it was estrangement, working through the rules, that threatened my being and so came to be clearly identified as estrangement; in this experience I realized just how utterly devastating estrangement really is.

Contradictory behavior results from estrangement

[14] We know that the rules are consistent, but I am full of contradictions and am locked up in my estrangement. [15] I refuse to own my thoughts, feelings, and actions. What I want to do, I don't; and what I hate, I do. [16] If my behavior is not in harmony with my desire, obviously I judge the rule as good. [17] This indicates just how separated I am from myself when I don't act the way I feel. [18] When I experience my contradiction so profoundly, I feel that I have no worth at all. I have the desire to perform but not the power. [19] My lofty ideals shatter on the rocks of my actual performance. [20] When I so completely contradict myself, the seriousness of my estranged condition is evident. [21] It seems the rule that when I will one thing, I do the very opposite. [22] For example, I really desire the purpose of God in the depth of my being, [23] but I am aware of an opposing drive which contradicts the standards accepted by my mind and enslaves me in old behavior patterns which deny God.

[24] O schizophrenic man that I am, who will heal me of this split within my person? I am grateful to God that it will be through our Lord Jesus Christ. Until he does, I will remain in the contradiction of serving God in part of me and denying him in another.

Living in union with the Spirit

8 [1] Now there is no accusing voice nagging those who are united to Jesus Christ, that is, those whose lives are directed by the Spirit rather than by old attitudes and patterns. [2] The new principle of life which Christ revealed has liberated me from the rules that unveiled my estrangement and made me feel my very being threatened. [3] What the rules could not accomplish in us humans, God accomplished through his Son who shared our humanity. He kept his unity with God while overcoming human estrangement, thus revealing the way for us to be united with God. [4] The right relations the rules intended can now be achieved in us who live spontaneously out of the Spirit rather than rigidly according to rules.

[5] Living according to old attitudes and patterns means being captive to whimsical impulses and past conditioning, but those who live in a new relationship to God are directed by the Spirit. [6] To be captive to one's own impulses results in meaninglessness and despair, but to live spontaneously out of the Spirit means real life through the unity of your being. [7] The person set on following his impulses without a point of reference will contradict God's plan because he refuses to accept God as the center and source of his life, [8] and his approach to God will never create a right relationship. This kind of performance-oriented person can never fulfill God's intention.

[9] But you are no longer dominated by this self-justifying attitude because you are in union with the Spirit of Christ. Whoever doesn't have this union doesn't have a relationship with Christ at all. [10] But when you do have a relationship with Christ, the urge to overcome your estrangement through your own efforts is under control, and your spirit is truly free to direct your life. [11] In fact, as you live in union with the Spirit of God, even your physical body will experience something like the resurrection of Jesus Christ. [12] So, my friends, we don't owe anything to the old way of life to live according to its

dictates, because to do so means death. [13] However, when we control our human desires under the direction of the Spirit, we have a fuller, richer life.

[14] Those who are directed by God's Spirit are God's children, [15] because this Spirit you have received is not a spirit of rules, creating slavery and fear. No, you have received the Spirit of sonship which means that you can call God "Father, my dear Father." [16] By uniting with our own spirit, this Spirit confirms that we are God's children. [17] As God's children we are his heirs, fellow heirs with Christ; when we suffer as he did, we take courage because we will be fulfilled as he was.

Ultimate fulfillment and the Spirit

[18] I conclude, however, that the suffering which we presently experience is nothing in comparison to the ultimate fulfillment for which we are destined. [19] You see, the deepest yearning in the heart of the creation awaits the final unveiling of God's family. [20] The creation has been subjected to the consequences of man's sin, not by nature's own choice, but according to the economy of God, who has also planted in it the longing for fulfillment. [21] Ultimately nature too will be released from all the consequences of man's fall and will share in the freedom and fulfillment of the family of God. [22] For now, however, we are aware that all of nature (of which human nature is a part) groans and is in pain like a woman giving birth. [23] Even those of us in whom hope has bloomed by the Spirit, we too groan while we await ultimate fulfillment, the transformation of our physical being.

[24] We are rescued from despair, however, by our hope; but the evidence of our hope is not visible and if it were, it wouldn't be hope anyway. For when we actually see something we don't have to keep hoping for it. [25] But when we do hope for what is not presently visible to us, then we patiently wait for it. [26] In addition to hope, we also have the Spirit, who compensates for our inadequacies. For example, because we

[29

don't know the proper way to pray, the Spirit enables us to commune with God through our groans which are never formed into words. [27] And God who knows our true motivation understands the language of the Spirit because he requests for us what God wills. [28] In your distress consider this also: When we love God we can be assured that God will make everything we experience to fulfill his purpose for us. [29] He has had us in his mind and awareness from the beginning, and has destined us to be shaped by his Son, thus making him the first of many family members. [30] These same persons God called, and those whom he called he made right with himself; and those who are in a right relation with him have begun to experience fulfillment.

The wonder of Christ's love

[31] How then shall we Christians respond to the despair of human existence? By saying, "If God is for us, who can oppose us?" [32] If God didn't rescue his own Son from suffering but gave him for all of us, won't he now give us everything that we need with him? [33] Who on earth can make any accusation against God's family? It is God who acquits us. [34] Who can sentence us? Only Christ who died for us, rose for us, and in God's very presence prays for us. (And would one who has so given himself sentence us? NO!)

[35] What can separate us from the love of Christ? Will suffering, or distress, or persecution, or hunger, or need, or danger, or threat of death? [36] (Sometimes we feel like those who said, "For your sake we are killed all day; we are like sheep waiting for the slaughter.") [37] No, in all these circumstances we may live triumphantly through Christ's love. [38] I am utterly convinced that nothing in death, nor any circumstance of life, nor good or evil spiritual forces, nor governmental authorities, nor anything present, nor anything to come, [39] nor anything above us or anything beneath us—not

anything in creation can ever separate us from God's love which he gives us in Christ Jesus our Lord.

The chosen people

9 [1] As my life is in Christ, I am sharing my deepest feelings with you honestly and accurately, and I feel straight with myself through the Spirit on what I am about to say. [2] I carry a great concern in my heart that grieves me. [3] My grief is sometimes so constant that I could even wish myself separated from Christ if that would help my fellow Jews know him. [4] These Israelites have so many earmarks of being special to God: they have their contracts with God; they have received the rules; they were entrusted with the ministry of God; and, they are recipients of his promises. [5] Their fathers are actually the human ancestors of Christ who has supreme authority forever. (God be praised!)

[6] The Jews' rejection of Christ does not mean God's promise has been broken. Not all of Jacob's descendants are true Jews, [7] neither does their being Abraham's descendants make them his children. Recall God's promise to Abraham: "Your true descendants will come through Isaac." [8] So not all the human descendants of Abraham are his spiritual children. The children resulting from God's promise are his true spiritual descendants. [9] I refer to the promise God made: "I will come and Sarah will have a son."

[10] And, add to this instance God's intervention when Rebecca had conceived by our ancestor Isaac. [11] When the children were still in her womb, before they were accountable for their actions, God decided which would be the chosen person, so that his purpose might be determined not by human effort but by his own choice. [12] God's power to choose was revealed when, contrary to custom, he said, "The older will serve the younger." [13] The record also gives us God's word, "I have selected Jacob rather than Esau."

[31

¹⁴ Will we judge this action of God unfair? Not at all. ¹⁵ Remember, he said to Moses, "I will express forgiveness and compassion to whomever I choose." ¹⁶ So our relation to God is not according to our choices nor our efforts but according to God's decision to relate to us. ¹⁷ Pharaoh is still another illustration of God's freedom to choose. Of Pharaoh he said, "For this reason I called you into existence so that I could show my power in you and have my nature recognized throughout the earth." ¹⁸ God expresses himself to one person like Moses who responds, and to another like Pharaoh who resists.

God calls the non-Jews as well as the Jews

¹⁹ You Jews may wish to argue, "Why does God criticize us if our action is his choice? Who can resist him?" ²⁰ I ask you one simple question: "Who are you to argue with God?" Will the created say to the creator, "Why have you made me as I am?" ²¹ Take the illustration of a potter. Doesn't he have power over the clay to make one lump into a beautiful, perfectly formed container and another into something which is blemished? ²² God could have made his rejection known to demonstrate his power. But he has endured patiently the containers which he could have destroyed (the non-Jews) ²³ so that he might reveal the depth of his being to the chosen vessels (the Jews) he created for fulfillment. ²⁴ He made this revelation of his nature for all of us whom he has called, not us Jews only but you non-Jews as well.

²⁵ Let me cite the prophets to you:

Through Hosea he said, "I will call a people who are not my people; and I will say, 'You are my beloved' to one who was not my beloved. ²⁶ And in the very place where it was said to them, 'You are not my people,' there they will be called the family of the living God."

²⁷ Isaiah warned the nation Israel, "Although the Jewish population becomes as numerous as grains of sand on the beach, only a portion of them will be preserved, ²⁸ because the

Lord will conclude his creation and rightly abbreviate his work to shorten his endeavor on the earth."

²⁹ Isaiah also said, "Except the Lord had chosen to leave a remnant, we would all have been destroyed like Sodom and Gomorrah."

³⁰ I have come to this conclusion. The non-Jews who had no relationship to God have received a right relationship to him through faith. ³¹ But the Jews who looked for a right relationship by keeping the rules have failed to keep the rules. ³² "Why?" you ask. Because they tried to achieve it through their own efforts and not through faith. They stumbled over the stumbling block. ³³ It is recorded, "I put down in Zion a stumbling block, a rock that will offend; and whoever accepts and trusts him will not be disappointed."

Why haven't the Jews responded?

10 ¹ Brothers and sisters, I deeply desire Israel's wholeness and pray to God for it. ² I am not implying they are unreligious; indeed, they have a zealous approach to God but not an informed one. ³ Because they are uninformed about God's way of relating to them, they busy themselves creating a superficial relationship. They have not received a true relationship with God as a gift.

⁴ For every person who believes, Christ terminates the rules as a way of relating to God. ⁵ Moses wrote about the person who lives by the rules. "The man who performs perfectly according to the rules will achieve a right relationship with God." ⁶ By contrast, the relationship we have received by faith says something like this: "Don't try to repeat by your performance what Christ has done— ⁷ like ascending to heaven or rising from death. ⁸ Look for the answer nearer by, even in your mouth and in the center of your being." I refer to the message of faith which I am preaching. ⁹ Here is my point in summary: "Verbally confess that Jesus is Lord and fully trust in your inner self that God brought him back to life, and you will be made whole." ¹⁰ You see, it is in your inner self that

you get rightly related to God through faith, and your verbal confession enables you to express for yourself and others the meaning of it.

[11] The record says, "Whoever trusts God will not be disappointed." [12] In this respect there is no distinction between the Jew and the non-Jew. The Lord who is over everyone will respond generously to anyone who requests his help. [13] Whoever makes the request will be made whole. But how can a person make such a request of an unknown friend? [14] How can one trust in a person he has never met? How will he meet him unless someone introduces them? [15] And how can a third party introduce them unless he has been commissioned to do that? What a beautiful calling, to introduce strangers to each other and to help good things happen to both! (That is how it is when you introduce a person to God.) [16] However, not every person you try to introduce to God will believe what you say about him. That is what Isaiah discovered when he lamented, "Lord, who has believed our report about you?" [17] In spite of this, though, trust is awakened by hearing an authentic confession of who Christ is and what he does.

[18] I ask, "Haven't my people heard about Christ?" Most assuredly, "Word of his action has spread across the earth and has echoed to the extremities of the earth." [19] Again, I ask, "Did Israel fail to recognize the message?" I reply, "Moses said, 'I will make you jealous by a people that are unrecognized, and with a nation of no consequence I will anger you.'" [20] Their guilt is sharpened by Isaiah's statement: "I was found by persons who did not look for me; I was shown to those who did not even request a look." [21] Of Israel God says, "For a long time I have offered myself to an unresponsive and unappreciative people."

God's love for the Jews

11 [1] After all this, I ask, "Has God completely rejected his people?" Not at all! I am Jewish, a member of Benjamin's clan, a descendant of Abraham. [2] God has not given up on me or on the nation he especially chose. Recall Elisha's prayer to God condemning Israel: [3] "Lord, they have murdered your messengers. They have demolished consecrated places. I alone remain, and they are looking for me to kill me." [4] And remember God's answer: "I still have seven thousand persons who have not bowed down to worship the false god." [5] Now just as then, there remains a faithful portion of the nation because God has chosen them through his unconditional love.

[6] If these remain in the family because of God's unconditional love, it is not due to their merit. If it were by their merit, it would be no longer by unconditional love. Where unconditional love prevails, merit ceases to exist. [7] The point of my argument is that the whole nation has not received God's promise, which it was looking for, but a small portion has and all the others have been blind to it. [8] There is a statement in our records that says, "God made them sleepy so that they dozed off and were unaware of the sights and sounds around them right to this very day." [9] Similarly, David said, "May their festivities be a snare, a trap, a stumbling block, and a type of retribution to them. [10] May they be blinded so they do not see and be burdened by the weight of their load."

[11] Has then the nation so gravely faltered that it will be completely rejected? Not at all. Through this temporary situation wholeness has come to non-Jews to stir up a spirit of jealousy in the Jews. [12] If the temporary setting aside of the Jews means fulfillment to the whole world and their failure means fulfillment to the non-Jews, what do you suppose it will mean when the Jews are reinstated? (Wow!)

A special word about the non-Jews

[13] Because I am a special messenger to non-Jews, a task I am proud of, I make a special appeal to you [14] hoping to get the Jews to follow your example so that perhaps some of them will be made whole. [15] Consider again, if setting them aside

[35

has resulted in the reconciliation of the whole world to God, what would their reinstatement mean? Why, it would mean the resurrection of the whole creation! [16] I am basing this affirmation on the principle that if the source is pure, then the derivatives from it are also pure. For example, if one piece of dough is leavened, the entire lump will be leavened, and if the root is good, so are the branches. [17] (Here is my warning to you non-Jews.) If some of the original branches of the olive tree were stripped off, and if you, like a wild olive branch, were inserted among the remaining branches and received from the root the nourishment of the olive tree, how can you harass the natural branches? [18] While you are harassing, remember—you do not sustain the root but the root sustains you.

[19] You may say, "The branches were stripped off so that I could be inserted." [20] You might consider that they were stripped off because of lack of trust and you yourself remain because of your trust; so do not become haughty but reverent. [21] If God would cut away the natural branches, you must never become presumptuous in your relation. [22] Keep in mind both the tenderness and hardness of God's actions. With the Jews he has acted firmly, but to you he expresses tenderness if you continue in your relationship. If you don't, your relationship too will die. [23] If they, on the other hand, relinquish their resistance to him, God will insert them again. He has the power to do just that. [24] If you non-Jews were cut from a wild olive tree and inserted contrary to nature in a cultured olive tree, how much easier it is to insert a natural branch into its own stock.

God's plan for Israel

[25] One thing I don't want you to lose sight of and become pseudointellectual and conceited—it's a situation I can't fully explain: the partial blindness of Israel has occurred only until

the non-Jews are admitted to God's family in full strength. [26] All Israel ultimately will be made whole. In our record it says, "Out of Zion the deliverer will come; he will strip away ungodliness from Jacob; [27] this is my contract with them when I take away their sins." [28] With respect to the good news they are antagonists, but this has resulted in something good for you. With respect to God's attitude toward them, they are still loved because God made a contract with their fathers, [29] and God's gifts and calling are irrevocable. [30] Make this comparison: it used to be that you did not believe God, but now through their lack of trust you have received forgiveness. [31] Now the Jews do not believe, but through the forgiveness being expressed to you they may eventually experience the same. [32] God saw all persons prisoners of unfaith so that he might forgive everyone of everything.

[33] O the intensity and the brilliance of both God's insight and knowledge! How impossible to explain his decisions or expose his motivations! [34] Who can say how God thinks? Who can give him advice? [35] Or, who has given to God before God has given, making him a debtor? [36] Because, you see, all creation emerges out of him; it is sustained by him; and it moves toward fulfillment in him. Through it all may God be fulfilled forever! Amen.

Guidelines on the Christian lifestyle

12 [1] With a vision, then, of the ultimate fulfillment of all things, I urge you, my brothers and sisters, to offer your whole self to God with no strings attached. Genuine worship is a reasonable response for you to make to him. [2] And don't pattern your life after the culture around you; rather, permit the Spirit of God within to transform your being and behavior by uniting your deepest thoughts and feelings with your actions so that you demonstrate God's intention which is positive, acceptable, and fulfilling.

[37

[3] Because of God's unconditional love for me, I introduce these suggestions to every one of you to help you live the Christian life:

Do not create a false image of yourself. Rather, honestly assess your personal worth in the light of your faith. [4] Just as our physical bodies have many parts and all these parts have their special functions, [5] so all of us are parts of the one body of Christ and because of that are part of each other. [6] We have varying functions according to the different gifts which God's unconditional love has bestowed upon us, so let us use them well. If we are speakers, let us speak in accordance with our confidence in that gift. [7] If we are servers, let us serve. If we are teachers, we should teach. [8] If we are encouragers, let us encourage. As givers let us give genuinely, without fanfare. Or as managers let us do so with dedication. When we help others let us do so cheerfully.

[9] Love without pretense. Resist evil; respond to good. Feel your love and express it to each other.

[10] Respect each other. [11] Conduct your affairs industriously; be alive with the Spirit; be attuned to your own spirit in serving the Lord.

[12] Celebrate your hope. Be patient when things don't work out. Keep on praying.

[13] Share with God's family who need your help, and practice hospitality.

[14] Affirm the worth of those who try to put you down. Affirm them, don't try to put them down harder.

[15] Celebrate with the celebrators and cry with the sad.

[16] Be as mindful of the other person's worth as you are of your own. Don't give special attention to celebrities and the wealthy, but recognize the unrecognized. Don't get conceited over what you know.

[17] Repay no one a put down for a put down. Think of those things that are good in your relations with all people.

[18] Do your utmost to live in harmony with everyone.

¹⁹ My beloved family, when anyone mistreats you, don't be obsessed with getting even with him; just drop it. Remember the record: "Leveling things is my business," says the Lord. "I will equalize."

²⁰ "If your enemy is hungry, give him food; if he is thirsty, give him a drink. By your actions you will reveal the contradiction in his behavior."

²¹ Do not be mastered by negative forces in the universe, but master them with positive action.

The Christperson's relationship to the government

13 ¹ I want each of you to respect the ruling authorities. All true authority originates in God, even the authority of the present government. ² To resist the rules of recognized authority is one way of resisting God, and such resistance requires discipline. ³ Rulers are no threat to the person doing good, only to the one doing evil. Do you want to be free from fear of the authorities? Then keep exhibiting good behavior and the authorities will affirm you. ⁴ Those in authority are servants of God for good. If your behavior is evil, you have a right to be afraid because the authorities will punish you. When they punish justly, they are executing God's justice. ⁵ Respect the authorities not out of fear but because such respect is your own value. ⁶ Pay your taxes because God's governmental agents deserve support. ⁷ Be responsible in all your duties: pay your taxes to the proper officials; reverence, respect, and honor them.

"Love your neighbor"

⁸ Do not let a claim exist against you except mutual love. Whenever you love a person, you have fulfilled your responsibility to him or her. ⁹ Take the rules against adultery, murder, stealing, coveting, for examples; these are fulfilled when you "love your neighbor as you love yourself." And, for that matter, the directive to "love your neighbor" fulfills every requirement

[39

regarding your relation to your neighbor. [10] So love fulfills the intent of the rule because it wills positive good to the neighbor.

[11] Be aware of this hour in history; open your eyes, for at this moment the time when perfect wholeness will be achieved is closer upon us than when we received the good news. [12] The night is nearly over; day is dawning. So let each of us strip off our night clothes and dress for the day. [13] Live an open life that you are willing for everyone to observe. Abstain from these practices: reveling, drunkenness, debauchery, vice, quarreling, and jealousy. [14] Adopt Christ's lifestyle as your model, a style which does not seek fulfillment by giving expression to every whim and urge.

Don't be judgmental about one another's beliefs

14 [1] Receive into your fellowship anyone who believes, even though his believing may be immature, but don't make it an occasion for disagreements about opinions. [2] For example, one person's faith permits him to eat anything he chooses while another, of immature faith, believes it proper to eat vegetables only. [3] In this instance, let the meat-eater not feel superior to the vegetarian, and the vegetarian not criticize the meat-eater. God has received both these persons. [4] What gives you authority to judge another man's employee? His employer determines whether or not he keeps him on the job. The vegetarian will be sustained in his relation to God because his actions are consistent with his knowledge.

[5] In a similar way one person regards one particular day as special. Another regards every day alike. With respect to special days, each person should have his own convictions. [6] The person who regards one day above others believes he honors God, and the person who affirms each day's importance alike does so with reverence for God. The same is true regarding what a person eats. The meat-eater celebrates life at the table because he offers thanks to God. The vegetarian also celebrates life and gives thanks to God.

[7] None of us is an island; we neither live nor die in isolation. [8] While we live, the Lord is the source of our being; when we die, the Lord is still the source of our being. Whether we live or die, our being is from the Lord. [9] For this very reason Christ died and came to life again, that he might be Lord of both the living and the dead. [10] Knowing this, why do you judge your brother's faith? Why do you try to wipe him out? God will ultimately evaluate each of us. [11] The record says, "Since I am the Lord, every knee will bow in reverence, and every tongue will confess allegiance to God." [12] At that time each of us will account to God for his behavior.

Make responsible love the standard for your decisions

[13] No longer render a final verdict on each other's behavior and thereby separate yourselves from a brother. Rather, decide against erecting barriers between yourselves or placing stumbling-blocks in each other's path to trip over. [14] I am convinced through my relationship to the Lord Jesus that no food is essentially unclean. However, if a person considers something unclean, it is unclean for him. But for another, who doesn't consider it unclean, it isn't. [15] But if your freedom to eat meat offends a fellow Christperson, ask yourself what decision love demands. Don't permit your freedom to destroy the confidence of a person for whom Christ died. [16] Don't let what you recognize as good be slandered. [17] Keep in mind the essential reality of the kingdom of God, which is not a matter of what you eat or what you drink, but right relationships, the unity of your being and joy through the Holy Spirit. [18] The person who serves Christ in these ways pleases God and is accepted by men and women.

[19] Let's strive, then, for a style of life which creates unity and builds wholesome relationships. [20] Don't let your freedom be destructive to God's work. Indeed, everything in creation is pure in its essence; yet to partake of certain things is de-

structive if it produces feelings of guilt in the person who eats it. [21] I consider it an act of love to abstain from eating meat or drinking wine or from anything which causes a brother to stumble, take offense, or become weak. [22] You have your own convictions about how to live, don't you? Apply these to yourself before God. Happy indeed is the person who can live by his deepest convictions without condemning himself for his choices. [23] The person who has questions about certain aspects of his behavior will feel guilty if he does those things because he is not acting in trust. All behavior which does not arise from trust is off course and separates us from God.

Accept each other, for God loves you all

15 [1] We who are mature in the faith should be sensitive to the insecurities of the immature and not only to our own desires. [2] I encourage you to respond to your neighbor's need for fulfillment and growth. [3] Christ, you know, was not motivated primarily by pleasure. He could have said of himself the old saying, "The rejection of those who have rejected you, I, too, have felt." [4] All those wise statements which were recorded before our time were written for our enlightenment, so that through the patience and encouragement received from them we may have hope for our lives. [5] May God, the source of patience and encouragement, enable you to have genuine community through Christ [6] so that in unity you may praise the God and Father of our Lord Jesus Christ.

[7] Accept each other as Christ has accepted each of us and thereby fulfill God's intention. [8] In order to demonstrate the faithfulness of God, Jesus Christ became a servant to the Jews and confirmed the promise God made to their fathers. [9] And, at the same time, he provided a basis for the non-Jews to praise God for his kindness. It is as if Christ were quoting the record, "I will confess your name in the midst of the non-Jews and there sing praise to your name." [10] Isaiah wrote, "Celebrate life with God's people, you non-Jews." [11] He also

said, "Offer praise to the Lord, all you non-Jews, and you Jews do likewise." [12] Once again Isaiah said, "There will be a descendant of Jesse who will rule the non-Jews, and they will place their confidence in him." (You see, God's inclusion of the non-Jews is no afterthought.) [13] May God, the source of hope, fill you with joy and unite you through your trust in him; and may your hope overflow through the power of the Holy Spirit.

Paul's work with the non-Jews

[14] I have a genuine confidence in you as fellow family members; you are essentially good; you know the meaning of your life; and you are able to instruct and admonish each other. [15] Nevertheless, because of the special call given me, I have chosen to write you quite boldly to refresh your thinking. [16] I am the special messenger of Jesus Christ to the non-Jews, interpreting the good news about God to them. I see myself in the role of presenting all non-Jews as an offering to God, an offering which I trust will be acceptable through the Holy Spirit.

[17] Through Jesus Christ I am proud of the results of my efforts to communicate God's love among the non-Jews. [18] I claim credit only for the fact that Christ has worked through me enabling the non-Jews to become obedient in both intention and performance. [19] In so doing I have experienced unmistakable evidence of his presence and some things he has done are beyond explanation, leaving me with wonder and amazement. With this kind of confirmation I have proclaimed the good news of Christ in every place from Jerusalem in the east to Illyricum in the west. [20] To this point I have endeavored to proclaim the good news to those who have never heard Christ's name, so that in each case I have laid my own foundation for the building I am constructing. [21] The record says, "Those who never heard of him will see, and those who had no knowledge of him will understand."

[43

Paul's plans for the future

[22] Because of my ministry in this virgin territory, I have been unable to visit you in Rome. [23] Since I have covered this area rather thoroughly, and because I have had for years such an intense desire to meet you, [24] I plan to visit you when I go to Spain. I hope to see you on my trip, to spend some time with you until I am filled for a time with your fellowship. [25] But now I must go to Jerusalem to assist God's people there. [26] You see, the Christpersons (non-Jewish) of Macedonia and Achaia have decided to send a contribution to assist the poor Christpersons in Jerusalem. [27] These non-Jewish Christpersons are pleased with this opportunity and rightly so since they have a debt to the Jews. If the non-Jews have become participants in their spiritual benefits, they have a responsibility to share their material goods with the Jews. [28] When I have completed this errand and have delivered this gift, I will come through Rome on my way to Spain. [29] And when I visit you, expect me to be celebrating life through the liberty I have received through Christ.

[30] I urge you, my brothers and sisters, because of what Christ has done and the love his Spirit generates, to join me in my struggle by praying to God for me. [31] Pray that I may elude the unbelieving Jews in Judea. Pray that the gift which I deliver to the Jewish Christpersons will be accepted with pleasure. [32] Pray that I may have a joyous visit with you by the will of God and that my own spirit will be renewed through your fellowship. [33] My prayer for you: "May the God who creates unity in all things be with you." Amen.

Personal greetings

16[1] I recommend to you Phoebe, our sister who holds office in the church at Cenchreae in Greece. [2] Receive her into your fellowship in the Lord as you would any Christperson and give her your assistance wherever she needs it. She has certainly been an encouragement to many persons, including me.

³ Greetings to Prisca and Aquila, who work side by side with me for Christ. ⁴ They have risked their lives for me and I am grateful to them (and not only I but the members of all the churches in non-Jewish territory). ⁵ Greetings to all the members of their house church.

⁶ Give Epaenetus a big hug—he was my first convert in Achaia, and I love him. Greet Mary, who worked so hard among you. ⁷ Greet Andronicus and Junias, my fellow Jews as well as my fellow prisoners. They are highly respected among the special messengers, and they were Christpersons before I was.

⁸ Greet Ampliatus, whom I love in the Lord. ⁹ Greetings to Urbanus, our helper in Christ's work, and Stachys, whom I love. ¹⁰ Greetings to Apelles, who is approved by Christ. Greetings to Aristobulus's entire family. ¹¹ Greetings to Herodion, my fellow Jew, and to those in the family of Narcissus who are Christpersons. ¹² Greetings to Tryphaena and Tryphosa, who work for the Lord. Greetings in love to Persis, who works hard for the Lord. ¹³ My greetings to Rufus, who seems specially chosen, and to his mother, who has been like a mother to me. ¹⁴ Greetings to Asyncritus, Phlegon, Hermes, Patrobas, Hermas, and the Christpersons with them. ¹⁵ Greetings to Philologus and Julia, Nereus and his sister, and Olympas, and all the Christpersons with them.

¹⁶ Greet each other with a warm embrace. All Christ's churches send you greetings.

One last word

¹⁷ I urge you, my fellow Christpersons, to identify those who create splits by teaching ideas which contradict what I have taught you and to avoid them. ¹⁸ These persons do not serve Christ but their own needs and wants. With their nice-sounding words and their enticing speech they deceive the uninformed.

[45

[19] Your own response to Christ has been talked about rather widely. I am glad for you and I want you to be full of knowledge about what is good—and quite uninitiated in evil. [20] And God who wills unity will crush the Adversary under your feet shortly. May the unconditional love of our Lord Jesus Christ be with you. Amen.

[21] Timothy, my fellow worker, and Lucius, Jason, and Sosipater, my fellow Jews, send greetings. [22] I, Tertius, who took dictation from Paul, send you greetings in the Lord's fellowship. [23] Gaius, who not only hosts me but the whole church, sends his greetings. Erastus, treasurer of this city, sends greetings as well as Quartus, a brother.

[25] Now to him who can enable you to stand firmly in the good news I have taught you through my presentation of Jesus Christ to you— [26] the interpretation of Christ which came to me through a revelation of God's secret that had been locked up since the dawn of creation but is now revealed; through sacred writings and under the direction of the eternal God, we spread this message to every nation so they may participate in the faith— [27] I say, "To God be ultimate fulfillment through Jesus Christ forever." Amen.

First Corinthians

INTRODUCTION

This first letter of Paul to the church at Corinth was written about 55 or 56 A.D. from Ephesus. (Actually, he had written a previous letter, but it has been lost to history.)

Corinth occupied a special place in Paul's ministry. He was the first Christian "special messenger" to go there (in 50 A.D.), and he stayed eighteen months, longer than anywhere else except Ephesus. Corinth, at that time the largest city in Greece, was exceptionally challenging for Paul because it was a city so full of vice and corruption. A cosmopolitan, wealthy seaport, it was also the home of a famous temple dedicated to the goddess Aphrodite, which housed hundreds of sacred prostitutes. This gives you some idea of what Paul was up against in trying to spread the good news and why immorality and idol-worship were two of the issues which most concerned him about the Corinthian church.

Paul's letter was prompted by reports he received of disharmony and immoral behavior among the Corinthian Christians. Also, his guidance had been sought on several crucial matters. The result was a letter that tied together a number of different threads.

Paul begins in chapter 1 with a call for harmony; he scorns the splinter groups that have sprung up—"Is Christ split into parts which contradict each other?"

In chapter 5 Paul deals with the immoral sexual behavior which he has heard about in the Corinthian church and underscores the

[47

need for discipline within the fellowship and guidelines for behavior (chapter 6).

One of the subjects the Corinthians solicited Paul's advice on is male-female relationships, and these he deals with in chapter 7. Another problem is whether or not to eat food that has been offered to idols. (chapter 8)

Other significant passages include worship responsibilities and the responsibility of Christian freedom (chapter 10); the gifts of the Spirit (chapter 12); the "love chapter" (13), probably one of the most famous chapters in the Bible; and the resurrection of Christ (chapter 15).

On the whole, while some parts of First Corinthians may seem irrelevant to twentieth-century readers, the major portion of this letter gives us an insight into the early Christian church and how Paul dealt with the practical problems which faced those first-century Christpersons.

FIRST CORINTHIANS

1 [1] I am Paul, called by God to be a special messenger of Jesus Christ. [2] My brother Sosthenes and I address this letter to the congregation at Corinth. You are Christpersons distinguished by your relation to him, and are becoming whole persons. Along with all persons who are being made whole, you recognize your need of a relationship with Jesus Christ as your Lord, just as we do. [3] May unconditional love and peace be with you from God our Father and our Lord Jesus Christ.

[4] I am constantly expressing my gratitude to God for you. I thank him for his unconditional love which he expressed to you in Jesus Christ, [5] who enriches your whole life as evidenced by your conversation and your knowledge. [6] The reality of what I have taught you about Christ is confirmed in your own experience, [7] and you do not lack any of his gifts while you await his appearance. [8] Christ will continue to measure up to what I have said until the end of history, when you will be without blame on that climactic day. [9] You can depend utterly and completely on God who invited you into a relationship with his Son, Jesus Christ our Lord.

Have harmony among yourselves

[10] My brothers and sisters, I beg you, in the name of Christ, come to agreement with each other to eliminate the barriers between you. Find a common perspective and adopt compatible values. [11] I have received a report from members of Chloe's family that you bicker with each other, that you have little groupings. [12] Some say, "We are Paul's disciples." Others say, "We are Apollos's followers." Still others claim Peter as their leader, and others Christ. [13] Let me quiz you. Is Christ split

[49

into parts which contradict each other? Was Paul nailed on a cross for you? Or were you baptized in Paul's name? [14] I'm glad I baptized only Crispus and Gaius [15] so they are the only ones who could make such a preposterous claim. [16] Oh yes, I did baptize Stephanas's family besides these. I don't recall any others. [17] No, Christ did not commission me to administer rites but to tell the good news in simple words, not in sophisticated rationalizations lest Christ's act for us be voided by my presentation.

The power and wisdom of God

[18] The story of Christ's offering himself on the cross sounds absurd to those who are dissipating their potential, but to us who are being made whole it is an unfailing source of God's power. [19] In the record God has said, "I will undermine the so-called wisdom of the wise and erase the understanding claimed by the prudent." [20] Point out to me the intellectual, the writer, the debater. Hasn't God made their so-called wisdom look foolish? [21] Yes, he wisely planned that his creatures by their own efforts could not discover him. He decided to use the absurdity of telling the story of the cross to make whole those who believe it. [22] The Jews want a supernatural miracle and the Greeks seek a logical answer, [23] but we keep telling them how God revealed himself through the death of Christ. [24] This event is a stumbling block to the Jews' expectations and is utterly foolish to the Greek way of thinking. But to those of us who have received God's love, both Jews and Greeks, the story of Christ demonstrates both the power and wisdom of God.

[25] Permit me to be a bit absurd. Even God's ignorance is more intelligent than man's wisdom; even his helplessness is stronger than man's strength. [26] Look at those persons in your fellowship. Few were educated in the schools, few hold political offices, few socially elite have responded to God's call.

²⁷ God has chosen an absurd way to stump the wise, a way of weakness to stop the powerful. ²⁸ He has chosen things without value, things that actually have been thrown away; he has chosen what does not exist to supersede what now exists. ²⁹ God has taken this seemingly contradictory path so that no person can boast to God about his abilities and achievements.

³⁰ But God himself has placed you in a relationship with Christ who is our source for everything—wisdom, right relations, wholeness, and ultimate fulfillment. ³¹ As the record states: "So if you must be proud, be proud of your relationship to him."

2 ¹ Friends, when I came to you, I did not present God's mystery as an orator or a philosopher. ² Before I arrived, I had already decided to speak only about Jesus Christ with a clear focus on his death on the cross and what that means for us. ³ Actually, when I was with you, I felt weak and full of anxiety to the point of shakiness. ⁴ In my talks I did not use seductive words based on human insight, but rather my words demonstrated the Spirit acting in potency ⁵ so that your faith was not grounded in human wisdom but in God's power.

⁶ As I think about it, I do share insights with those who are more mature. But my wisdom is not a worldly wisdom nor is it endorsed by those human authorities who will eventually lose their power. ⁷ Rather, I am proclaiming God's wisdom which still has an element of mystery in it, I mean that wisdom which was buried deep in his mind at the dawn of creation. ⁸ None of the earthly authorities knew this wisdom; if they had, they would not have nailed the source of creation's fulfillment to a cross. ⁹ The record reads, "No eye has seen, no ear has heard, nor has it ever entered man's awareness what God has in store for those who love him." ¹⁰ While we cannot explore this mystery by our own intellect, God has unveiled it by his Spirit. The Spirit penetrates everything, even the secrets hidden deep in the mind of God.

[51

How the Spirit enables us

[11] What person can understand all the impulses and urges of the human heart apart from the human spirit? Even so, the nature of God cannot be discovered by humans—yet God's Spirit knows it. [12] We Christpersons have not received mere human insight; we have been given the Spirit of God. The Spirit enables us to recognize both God's activity and his gifts. [13] We talk about our spiritual perceptions not in the logic of the academy but in new symbols which the Spirit inspires. We discuss the action of God in our lives, and the symbols we use participate both in God's action and in our experience of it.

[14] The person without the Spirit, however, is not aware of God's action. Even a discussion of the matter sounds foolish to such people. They cannot discern God's actions because only people in tune with the Spirit can see and understand them. [15] By contrast, people with God's Spirit can discern and evaluate everything, yet they themselves cannot be fully evaluated. [16] For (as the record reads), "Who has fully understood God's mind? Who can counsel him?" As spiritually alive persons, we think in our context the kinds of thoughts that Christ did.

3 [1] But my friends, I can't write to you as spiritually alive, mature persons. I keep reminding myself of your immaturity; you are infants in your relation to Christ. [2] In the realm of spiritual development, I had to feed you with milk like a baby because till now you have been unable to handle solid food, and evidently you are still not ready—[3] you are still so immature. You compete against each other; you build walls between yourselves. Isn't this immature behavior? Isn't this how persons function who are unrelated to Christ? [4] As long as you divide yourselves into groups—a Paul group and an Apollos group, for example—you betray your immaturity.

What it means to work with God

[5] Just who do you think Apollos is? Or Paul, for that matter? We are only agents who shared the good news with you and

you believed it. Why, God has made every person an agent for him. ⁶ Look at it like this. I planted the seed, Apollos watered it, and God caused the seed to grow and bear fruit. ⁷ Planting and watering are nothing in comparison with the power to cause growth. ⁸ The agents in planting and watering are both human beings, and each will be rewarded for his constructive efforts. ⁹ We are co-workers with God. You are God's garden or God's building.

¹⁰ I have used the skills which God in his unconditional love gave me. As a skillful builder I have poured a firm footing, yet another craftsman builds on it. (Let every builder follow carefully to the specifications.) ¹¹ No other foundation will be poured than the one which I have already poured—Jesus Christ. ¹² Numerous materials may be used to build on this foundation—gold, silver, jewels of all kinds; wood, grass, and straw. ¹³ Builders beware! There will come a day when the quality of your construction will be exposed. It will be tested by fire (imagine what will happen to the wood, grass, and straw!). ¹⁴ If a builder's construction is fireproof, he will be rewarded. ¹⁵ His construction may be gutted by the flames, however, while he himself is rescued, in a narrow escape.

Find fulfillment in God, not others

¹⁶ Be aware that you are God's house and the Spirit of God lives in you. ¹⁷ If a person abuses the dwelling place of God, he will die an early death. The place in which God lives is sacred, and you are that place.

¹⁸ Don't play games with yourself. If anyone in your fellowship gets puffed up with pseudowisdom, let him empty his head so that he can be filled with the truth. ¹⁹ Human efforts to find fulfillment in human cultural patterns are absurd to God. ²⁰ The record says, "God captures the pseudointellectuals in their own arguments." Also, "The Lord recognizes the emptiness of their thoughts."

²¹ In conclusion I admonish you: "Don't look for ultimate

[53

fulfillment in other persons. You already have everything. [22] You have Paul and Apollos and Peter. You have the world and life and death. You have the present and the future. [23] In fact, everything belongs to you and you belong to Christ who belongs to God."

4 [1] In respect to my discussion about how to regard us leaders, you should consider us subordinates to Christ, as managers of God's revelation of himself. [2] The chief requirement of a manager is faithfulness.

[3] I am not the least concerned with the fact that you are deciding what is right and what is wrong with me . . . and even passing sentence on me. Neither you nor anyone else can put me down unless I first put myself down. (And I'm not doing that.) [4] But though I don't know of anything against me, my ignorance doesn't mean I am correct in my appraisal because the final evaluation is in God's hands. [5] Therefore, I am suggesting that none of us make premature judgments about ourselves or others. Wait until that final appearance of the Lord when he will uncover the hidden parts of our lives and reveal our true motives. When the whole truth is known, every person will receive proper recognition from God.

What does it mean to be a special messenger?

[6] My friends, I have compared Apollos and me to farmers and carpenters so that you can see more accurately the role we play in God's work. Learn from our example not to put human beings in places of false authority, or to allow division to come about through jealousy. [7] You are unique, but what is the source of your distinctiveness? What do you possess of true worth that was not a gift? If you received it as a gift, why do you boast as though you earned it?

[8] You are fulfilled. You are wealthy. You have reigned like kings without help from me. (I'm speaking sarcastically.) I really wish you were in charge of things so that I might share your authority. You seem to think that we consider being

God's special messengers makes us persons of repute. Let me give you my inside evaluation. [9] It seems to me we are at the bottom of the list, like men waiting for execution. To myself I often appear to be an object of ridicule for the whole universe, for angels and for humans like you.

[10] Let me contrast your plight with ours. We are considered simpletons for Christ, but you are wise in him. We are weak but you are strong. You have a place of recognition but we are rejected. (More of my sarcasm.)

[11] At this moment God's special messengers need life's simple necessities: food, drink, and clothing. We are handled roughly and have no home of our own. [12] We work at a trade to pay our expenses. When we are put down, we try to lift others up; when we are treated unjustly, we accept it; [13] when our reputation is attacked, we offer a clear statement of who we are. Yet to this day we are treated like human leftovers fit only to be thrown in the garbage.

Words from a "father" to his "children"

[14] I am not describing our plight to embarrass you, but as my children I want to warn you. [15] Though you may have ten thousand teachers in the faith, you have only one father. I am your father, and through Christ Jesus you are my children through the good news I shared with you. [16] As my children, then, follow me like a father.

[17] And because you are my children, I have sent you my beloved and faithful son in the Lord, Timothy. He will help you recall my instruction and my example which are the same in every congregation everywhere. [18] I know that some of you are getting big-headed because you think I am not going to visit you personally. [19] But if God wills, it won't be long before I will be coming to see you, and when I arrive, I want to hear not only the words of the big-headed but how it really is with them in their lives. [20] The authentic expression of God's intention does not consist of words disconnected from feelings

and values, but actions in harmony with reality. [21] Tell me, when I visit do you want me to come like an angry father with rod in hand, or shall I come with the gentleness of a nurse?

Disciplining the fellowship

5 [1] When I visit you, I will deal quite honestly with you because I have a report that you have a case of immoral sexual behavior. I am referring to the man who is having intercourse with his stepmother. Even non-Jews don't do that kind of thing. [2] It saddens me that you are haughty about this instance rather than distressed. You ought to do something to discipline these persons. [3] Although I haven't talked with the couple or with any of you personally, I have already decided what must be done. [4] When you meet in fellowship, and the presence of Christ is evidenced (and my spirit also), by the power of our Lord Jesus Christ [5] this man must be handed over to the Adversary to experience the painful consequences of his behavior so that he will be ultimately fulfilled through our Lord Jesus Christ.

[6] Your boastful attitude is not at all commendable. You recall the old saying, "A little yeast spreads all through the dough." [7] Get rid of this old yeast, the leavening that is wielding so much influence in your fellowship, so that you may be pure, without any yeast at all, just as you are in reality, as Christpersons. You can see that I am using the unleavened bread of the Passover as a metaphor. Actually, Christ has given himself to become our bread. [8] Let us then celebrate the festival not with the leavening, the behavior and attitude of our previous lives, but with our new life, which is without pretense and grounded in reality.

[9] In a previous letter I asked you not to associate with persons engaging in sexual relations with a person to whom they are not married. [10] I did not mean for you to avoid non-Christians who have sex promiscuously or those who are

greedy to grasp all they can or swindlers or idolators (all of whom lack a basic commitment). If you tried to avoid contact with all these persons, then you would have to remove yourselves from this world.

[11] In this letter I am writing you to exclude from your fellowship a brother or a sister who is behaving like a non-Christperson. I am referring to Christpersons who still try to grab all they can get, to those who worship the created as the Creator, to those who undermine the character of others, to those who cheat. At this time I ask you not to affirm the behavior of persons like these by including them in your fellowship. [12] But as for those outside the fellowship, what right does any of us have to condemn them? That is God's affair. [13] But are we leaders not responsible for disciplining those within the fellowship? Of course. So, discipline the person to whom I have referred.

Settling disputes within the fellowship

6 [1] The matter of passing judgment within the fellowship brings up another issue. How can you Christpersons take your arguments to judges who are not Christpersons for a decision and not to members of Christ's community? [2] Aren't you aware that we Christpersons will eventually judge the whole world? If you eventually will have such a weighty responsibility, why can't you settle inconsequential disputes today? [3] Furthermore, don't you know that we will judge heavenly messengers? How much more should we be able to evaluate properly a few earthly concerns. [4] If you have disputes concerning vital issues in your lives, even the least esteemed person in your fellowship should be able to settle it.

[5] I suppose I am trying to shame you when I ask: "Isn't there one arbitrator in your fellowship? Not even one person who can settle a dispute between two brothers?" [6] One brother goes to court against another requesting a decision from a non-

Christian judge. [7] What a shame that you resort to such a practice. Why—why, it would be better to accept injustice, and even allow someone to take advantage of you. [8] Consider the witness you make when you treat each other unjustly or fraudulently and then request a judgment from a non-Christian.

Guidelines for behavior

[9] You need to change your behavior. You may be assured that those who have snarled relationships will not enter into a positive relationship with God. Don't delude yourselves. None of these persons express God's intention: those who have sex without commitment, worshipers of the created, those who break their commitment to their mates, homosexuals, [10] those who take the property of others (and those who want to), excessive drinkers, character assassinators, cheats—none of these fulfills God's destiny for them. [11] And some of you lived lives like that—but you have been cleaned up, you have been made whole, you have been given a right relationship with God through Jesus Christ by the action of God's Spirit in you.

[12] With regard to my behavior, there are no rules against anything I wish to do, but everything I may consider doing is not for my highest good. I have permission to do anything I choose, and I choose not to become enslaved by anything I do. [13] You have a saying, "Food is for the stomach, and the stomach for food." True, but both food and stomachs will eventually decay. For example, just because you are capable of sex, that doesn't mean you should have intercourse with whomever you please. Your body is made for the Lord, who cares about your needs. [14] And God raised our Lord from death, and that same power will raise us. [15] Are you not aware that your bodies are part of Christ? Can you picture bodies which are part of Christ becoming part of a call girl? [16] You realize, don't you, that anyone having intercourse with a call girl is united to her. The record says, "The two shall become united." [17] But the

person united to the Lord is united to him in spirit, and that is what you are destined for.

[18] So turn away from sex outside marriage. No other sin affects your body in quite the same way as sex with someone to whom you are not committed. [19] Keep clearly in your thinking that your body is the home of God's Spirit who even now lives in you as God's visitor. The source of your being is not within yourself; that is a gift from God through what Jesus did for you. [20] So choose to fulfill the intention of God in your body and in your spirit which are his.

Should you marry?

7 [1] You have written to me requesting my advice on male-female relationships. Because our present social structures are temporary, it is wise to avoid marriage. [2] But to have sexual relations outside marriage is destructive, so go ahead and marry and be loyal to your partner. [3] Men, satisfy the sexual needs of your wives; and wives, you do the same for your husbands. [4] A woman cannot satisfy her own sexual needs by herself, nor can a man satisfy his alone; each is fulfilled by the other. (Masturbation is a poor substitute for intercourse.) [5] Don't withhold sex from each other unless you agree to abstain for spiritual reasons. After the agreed-upon time, express your sexual feelings to each other so that you won't be tempted to express them to someone else.

[6] I am not issuing a command now, but making a concession. [7] I wish all of you were single like me, but I realize that each of us has his own gift from God; some are to marry and others are not. [8] I hope you unmarrieds and widowed will remain as I am. [9] If, however, you can't control your sex drive, it is better for you to marry than to burn with passion. [10] And, I command—no, the *Lord* commands—a wife must not run off from her husband. [11] If she does separate from him, I hope she too will remain single or settle her differences with her husband. Also, no husband should be irresponsible to his wife.

Marriage between Christians and non-Christians

¹² I have something to say to the rest of you. (Now this is Paul speaking, not the Lord.) If a Christian man is married to a non-Christian woman and she desires to live with him, he should not divorce her. ¹³ Likewise, for the Christian woman married to the non-Christian man, if he wants to live with her, let her not divorce him. ¹⁴ If a husband or wife is a believer, there is a sense in which the spouse who is not a believer is consecrated to God. Otherwise, the children would be tainted. But as it is, they are consecrated to God. ¹⁵ However, if an unbelieving spouse decides to leave, permit him or her to go. In this instance a Christperson is not under necessity to keep the marriage together. God wills us to be united with ourselves and each other, and perpetuating such a conflicting relation does not create unity. ¹⁶ If you can constructively maintain a mixed marriage, who knows but what the wife will be redemptive in the life of her husband or the husband in the wife.

Don't change your life situation

¹⁷ Because of the uncertainty of these times, live in whatever state you find yourself. This is the rule which I have established in all the congregations. ¹⁸ If you were not circumcised as a physical initiation when you became a Christian, then don't have it done now. ¹⁹ It doesn't matter whether you have this rite or not. Loving God, your neighbor, and yourself is what really counts. ²⁰ I emphasize—don't change your life situation. Keep things as they were when you became a Christperson. ²¹ Were you a slave when you became a Christperson? Don't fret over it. If you have an opportunity to obtain your freedom, do it. ²² For when slaves become Christpersons, the Lord sets them free, and those who are free become slaves to Christ when they become Christpersons. ²³ Just remember that Christ has purchased your freedom, so don't ever see yourselves as slaves to men. I repeat my message again. ²⁴ Because

of the times in which we live, remain in the situation you were in when you became a Christperson.

More thoughts on marriage

[25] I don't have a direct word from the Lord for those who have never married, but as one who because of God's mercy is reliable, I urge them to remain as they are. [26] This is good advice because of the distressing circumstances in which we find ourselves. [27] Are you committed to a mate? Don't break the commitment. Are you free? Don't join yourself to a mate. [28] If you marry, however, you have committed no wrong; a virgin who marries is not doing wrong. If you do marry, you will face distressing circumstances, and I am trying to help you avoid them.

[29] My Christian friends, it appears to me that our time on this earth is brief. If you have spouses, you may have to act as though you didn't. [30] If you have cause to weep, you may have to ignore it; or cause to rejoice, you may have to ignore that, too. [31] You may purchase goods, never to have them delivered; you may make plans, never to execute them. The present structures of this world are crumbling.

[32] I want you to live without anxiety. When you are unmarried, you are free to devote all your energy to Christian concerns and fulfilling the Lord's intention. [33] If you are married, you must make a living and be responsible for your wife —how you can fulfill her needs. [34] An unmarried woman is free to devote herself to Christian concerns with her whole spirit and body, but a married woman must consider family responsibilities and the needs of her husband. [35] I have made these suggestions to help you. I have no desire to control or manipulate you, but to encourage order and to enable you to discover the lifestyle that is appropriate for serving God without distraction.

[36] Even in these uncertain times, if you are getting too intimate with the woman you are dating and feeling guilty be-

[61

cause of your actions, or if your friend is beginning to feel unattractive and cheated, go ahead and marry. [37] On the other hand, if you can control your sexual desire and refrain from sex by your free choice, you are better off. [38] So then, it's all right to marry but better not to.

[39] A woman is legally bound to her husband as long as he is alive. When he dies, she is released from that law and is free to remarry as the Lord directs. [40] But I still maintain she will be happier not to marry, and I believe God's Spirit is directing me when I make this statement.

Be prudent about eating food offered to idols

8 [1] All of us are in the know about the food which has been offered as a sacrifice to an idol. (It occurs to me that we can let the accumulation of data give us a false and inflated self-image, but love gives us balance. [2] If you think of yourself as superintelligent, you don't have the knowledge that is really important. [3] If you love God, he recognizes you and that's what I consider important.)

[4] Now let's get back to the matter of eating food which was first offered to a pagan god. We know that the pagan god has no lasting significance in the scheme of things because there is only one God. [5] Even though many objects may be called god in heaven or on earth (as indeed they are called gods and lords), [6] to us Christpersons there is only one God, the Father, and he is the source of all creation and the goal of our lives. There is only one Lord, Jesus Christ, who is God's sole agent in creation—even we came into existence through his act.

[7] Not every person recognizes this principle. I know that some do not because when they eat the meat of an animal which was first offered to a pagan god, they feel guilty as if they themselves are worshiping that god. [8] Meat in itself doesn't affect our relationship with God, not even meat from a pagan altar. If we eat it, we are not any better; if we don't eat it, we are no worse. [9] But I urge you to use this freedom

wisely so that you do not offend a Christperson who lacks this maturity.

¹⁰⁻¹¹ Your freedom may be misinterpreted by a brother or sister. Suppose a new Christperson who is still bound up in the rules observes you eating in a pagan temple; your behavior may be destructive to him or her, a person for whom Christ died. Other Christpersons may be unable to accept your freedom, the result being an overwhelming sense of doubt and even their dropping out of the fellowship. ¹² When your freedom destroys a fellow Christperson, you are really violating Christ. ¹³ So I have concluded that if exercising my freedom to eat pagan food in pagan temples destroys a brother or sister, I will never eat it. Love takes charge of freedom.

Paul defends himself from his critics

9 ¹ I am feeling under attack, so I will remind you of several facts. I most assuredly am a special messenger of Jesus Christ. I am free to do and be what he intended. I have even seen Jesus Christ. You yourselves are evidence of my special call. ² I may not be recognized as a special messenger by others, but how can you deny it? The fact that you are Christpersons confirms my special call.

³ Having underscored my special call, now permit me to answer the criticisms being leveled against me. ⁴ Isn't it proper for me to have the food and drink that I need? ⁵ Would it not be proper also for me to take a wife or a sister with me on these trips like the other special messengers and the Lord's brothers and Peter? ⁶ Why must Barnabas and I alone work at a trade to pay our expenses? ⁷ While you ponder these questions, consider these also: What soldier pays his own expenses? What farmer is forbidden to eat the food he raises? What dairyman is refused milk from his herd?

⁸ Please do not think that these ideas are of human origin. ⁹ Recall Moses' statement: "You must not muzzle the ox which tramples the wheat to separate it from the stalk." ¹⁰ Does God

[63

will that the needs of an ox be met and not ours? Surely he had us in mind when he said, "The person who cultivates a crop should do so in hope; and, the one who gathers should gather in hope of a share of the harvest."

[11] If I have freely sown the good news of God's love among you, is it absurd to you for me to reap some financial help for my work? [12] You support the ministry of others; should not I have a place of priority in your giving since I first gave the good news to you? Even though I have this right, I have never asked you for a penny for fear I should dilute the power of Christ's good news. [13] Don't you realize that Jewish priests who work in the temple are supported by offerings? After the priests have offered the sacrifices, they later eat the food. [14] The Lord commanded that those who proclaim the good news should receive a living from their ministry.

[15] I could have used all these arguments and illustrations to get you to support me, but I haven't. And, even now I'm not writing you to request a contribution. I would rather die than let anyone destroy my claim that I have always proclaimed the good news without pay. [16] Even though I proclaim the good news, I can't take credit for my efforts because I am so sure that I was destined to do this work. I would contradict my identity should I do anything else. [17] If I accept my call willingly, I am rewarded both with fulfillment now and with the hope of ultimate fulfillment; but if I proclaim the good news unwillingly, then I have still been entrusted with this assignment. What good is that?

Proclaiming the good news effectively

[18] So when I proclaim the good news, I do so without any charge. I don't make full use of my right to receive payment. [19] I am under the dictates and directions of no person, but I have made myself a slave to everyone so that I may communicate with more persons. [20] I have tried to identify with every person: to Jews I became like a Jew to communicate

better with them; to those living under the law, I became a person under the law—even though I was not under the law—to communicate better with them; [21] to those outside the law, I became like them (I don't mean lawless because I was under the law of Christ's love) so that I could communicate on their wavelength; [22] with the weak, I identified my own weakness so that we could meet on the same ground. I have placed myself in the same circumstances of everyone to whom I have tried to communicate the good news, so that my message might be heard by more, causing some to be made whole. [23] And I make these identifications because of the good news so that I may participate in its benefits.

[24] You are aware that in track meets, all the participants in a race run, but only one is the winner. We should all *run like a winner*. [25] Everyone who strives to be a winner disciplines his whole life. Now athletes train to receive a reward that doesn't last, but we train to receive one that is permanent. [26] So I run with my eye on the goal, I land every punch where it will count, [27] and I keep all my desires under control, to avoid the possibility that while I have urged others to discipline themselves, I myself should lose out completely.

Learning from the examples of others

10 [1] My brothers and sisters, I remind you of the experiences of our forefathers and their families. All of them traveled in the shadow of the cloud and all passed through the Red Sea; [2] all had a baptism of sorts by Moses in the cloud and in the sea; [3] all ate the spiritual food and drank the spiritual water which God provided. [4] They all drank from that spiritual rock —and that rock symbolized Christ. [5] Though they shared in common these spiritual experiences, a number of them did not fulfill God's intention, and as a consequence they died during their wanderings in the desert.

[6] Their experiences serve as a model for us, teaching us that we should not give in to our ravenous appetites, which do not

fulfill God's intention for us. ⁷ Let none of us give supreme devotion to the created world as some of our forebears did. The record states, "They stuffed their stomachs and entertained themselves." ⁸ Let us not engage in immorality as did a large number of them. (Recall that twenty-three thousand were wiped out as a consequence of their undisciplined behavior.) ⁹ Let us not experiment with the power of God as some of them did who were bitten by snakes for their irreverent behavior. ¹⁰ Let us not give ourselves to grumbling and complaining as did those Israelites who were destroyed by the Adversary. ¹¹ All their experiences are examples for us who are participating in the climax of history, teaching us how to conduct our lives.

¹² If you think that you have all your desires under control, beware of losing your grip. ¹³ Be confident of one thing: no testing will come your way which has not been experienced by other human beings. In every situation God is utterly dependable. He will permit no test beyond your endurance, and when you are tested he will provide a way to endure it.

Some worship responsibilities

¹⁴ My dear friends, in your worship do not substitute anything for God. ¹⁵ I am appealing to your reason; make your own judgment about what I have to say. ¹⁶ When we consecrate the communion wine and drink it, we participate in the blood of Christ, don't we? When we break the communion bread and eat it, aren't we participating in the body of Christ? ¹⁷ We are united when we eat this bread; we become one body by partaking of the one bread.

¹⁸ Let me illustrate. When Jewish people eat their sacrificial food, don't they become identified with what the altar represents? Now apply the same principle to non-Jews. ¹⁹ Am I saying that false gods have reality and thus offerings to them have merit? No, quite the contrary. ²⁰ I am saying these sacri-

fices are offered to God's adversaries, not to him, and I don't want you Christpersons expressing unity with God's adversaries. ²¹ You cannot eat at the Lord's table and at the table of his enemies. You cannot be simultaneously in fellowship with his family and that of the Adversary. ²² Are we provoking God to jealousy? Are we stronger than he is?

Be responsible in your freedom

²³ You may argue, "But there are no rules against anything I wish to do." I answer, "Yes, but not everything is for your highest good." Again, you say, "But all things are all right for me." "Yes, but not everything enables you to fulfill God's intention." ²⁴ Don't consider your own needs and wishes only. Consider what is good for your neighbor.

²⁵ Whatever is sold at the market, eat, but don't ask any questions about it for the sake of your conscience. ²⁶ Just remember, "The earth belongs to the Lord and *everything* in it." ²⁷ If one of your non-Christian friends invites you to a party and you want to go, eat what is offered you without question. ²⁸ If during the party someone announces, "This meat was first offered to one of the gods," don't eat it for his sake and for conscience's sake. ²⁹ I say "for his sake" because by eating he could think you approved a pagan god. If such were the case, you might feel guilty that you had falsely represented yourself to your host. You ask, "Why is my freedom limited by another person's view of reality? ³⁰ If through God's unconditional love I am free to eat this meat offered to pagan gods, why am I accused when I celebrate my freedom?" (A good question!) ³¹ Whatever you choose to do in your freedom, let your choices be determined by God's ultimate fulfillment.

³² Try not to cast a stumbling block in the path of anyone: neither Jew nor non-Jew nor the family of God, ³³ just as I try to get the affirmation of all these persons by not seeking

personal gain, because I want as many as possible to be made whole. [11:1] And I want you to pattern your lives after me just as I pattern mine after Christ.

An explanation about certain traditions

11 [2] I affirm you, my friends, for the careful way that you keep me in mind and follow the directives I gave you. [3] Regarding priority, consider Christ as the source of humanity and, in the creation of humanity, man as the source of woman historically, and God as the source of Christ eternally. [4] Given this context, our leaders have decided that a man performing a religious function (like praying or witnessing) with his head covered is impolite. [5] But a woman performing a similar function with her head uncovered is equally impolite. [6] A woman ought to cover her head. And, if your women refuse to cover their heads, let them shave themselves. [7] A male should not cover his head because he images God's fulfillment just as females image the fulfillment of males (and vice-versa).

[8] In respect to time the man was first created, then the woman. [9] Originally, as the story goes, woman was created for man's fulfillment. [10] If you look at this order of things, a woman should cover her head as a sign of respect to man.

[11] While I am in the act of describing how we have viewed the order of creation, it occurs to me that in the Lord, man and woman are mutually dependent on each other. [12] Just as the woman originated from the man in the creation story, since then man has come from the woman. Man and woman, like everything else, have their origin in God. [13] Why don't you make your own decision about whether or not a woman should cover her head when she prays? [14] It seems to me that even nature teaches us that it is impolite for a man to have long hair. [15] But on the contrary, a woman's long hair gets her recognition because it covers her head. [16] However, if any person in your fellowship gets argumentative about long hair, we

don't recognize any other practice; neither do any of the congregations of God.

A warning about some undesirable practices

[17] While there has been much for which I could affirm you, you have some uncommendable practices. You are in a worse condition after you meet for worship than before you meet. [18] For one thing, I hear that you argue and bicker at your meetings—and I partially believe it. [19] There is a major problem in your fellowship, namely, that each time you meet you begin judging who is worthy to participate in the fellowship and who is not. [20] The result is that when all the members of the fellowship congregate in a single place, it is impossible for you to celebrate the Lord's Supper. [21] When you begin the celebration, one person is loading his plate while another is left hungry and still another is getting drunk on the communion wine. [22] Can't you pitch this kind of party in your own homes? Your greedy, undisciplined behavior is evidence that you despise God's people, as well as putting the poor to shame. How can I respond to this malpractice? I certainly cannot commend you.

Celebrating the Lord's Supper properly

[23] I have received from the Lord how the supper should be celebrated, and I have passed that on to you. You recall that the Lord Jesus, on the night of his betrayal, took a piece of bread, [24] gave thanks to God for it, broke it in pieces, and said to his disciples, "Take a piece, knowing this represents my body which is given for you. Eat it and remember what I have done for you." [25] In similar fashion, when the supper had ended, he took a cup of wine and said, "This cup represents the new contract which I will ratify through offering my life. Whenever you drink this, drink it remembering what I have done." [26] As often as you eat this bread and drink this wine, you declare Christ's death until he comes again.

[69

²⁷ But whoever partakes of the Lord's Supper unworthily commits a crime against Jesus himself. ²⁸ Therefore, each of you should examine your feelings and your behavior before celebrating the Lord's Supper. ²⁹ A person eating and drinking without recognizing how sacred the Lord's body is, brings condemnation upon himself. ³⁰ I believe this insensitivity is the reason that some of you are weak and sickly and some have died. ³¹ How much better it would be if we evaluated our own behavior and corrected our own actions! Then we should not be judged ourselves. ³² When we refuse to take responsibility for ourselves, the Lord disciplines us so that we will not be finally rejected like the rest of the world.

³³ When you gather to celebrate the Lord's Supper, wait for each other. ³⁴ And if any of you feels starved, eat before you leave home so that you will not need to gorge yourself at the celebration, thus condemning yourself. The other problems you have regarding the Supper, I will straighten out upon my arrival.

Gifts of the Spirit

12 ¹ My friends, I do not want you to be confused about gifts of the Spirit. ² Let me remind you, first, of your background: you used to be non-Jews getting direction for your lives from idols which could not make a sound. But I want to be very clear on one point. ³ No person can curse Jesus Christ by the inspiration of the Spirit of God, neither can anyone confess that Jesus is the Lord except through the inspiration of the Holy Spirit. (So as Christpersons, you have received the inspiration of the Spirit.)

⁴ There are various gifts, but they are all from the same Spirit. ⁵ There are different ways these gifts may be used, but the same Lord directs their functioning. ⁶ And different results are effected from their functioning, but the same God works through them all for everyone. (I am underscoring the fact

that these gifts have a common source, direction, and purpose and they should not cause division.)

[7] A particular gift of the Spirit is given to each Christperson to benefit the whole family of God. [8] To one person the Spirit gives the communication of special insights; the same Spirit gives to another knowledge; [9] to another a special capacity for trust; to another the gift of enabling people to be healed; [10] to another the privilege of being a channel of God's miraculous power; to another witnessing the good news; to another the ability to distinguish between good and evil spirits; to another ecstatic utterances; and still to another the translation of these sounds into meaning. [11] All these special gifts are to function in unity because they originate from the Spirit who gives them to each person as he chooses.

The unity of the body

[12] Let me use the body as an analogy. The body is a unit that has many parts or organs, all of which form a common body. This illustrates the functioning of the Body of Christ. [13] One Spirit immerses us into this Body whether we are Jews or non-Jews, servants or free persons; all of us in the Body have experienced the Spirit in common. [14] The physical body has more than one part; in fact, it has many parts. [15] If a foot says, "Because I can't work like a hand, I'm not part of the body," does that silly assertion make it so? [16] If the ear says, "Because I can't function like an eye, I'm not part of the body," does that make it true? [17] Suppose the whole body was made up of one eye (just picture that), how could it hear? Or if the whole body were an ear, how could it smell? [18] These absurd questions should help you understand that God has created the various parts of the body and made them complementary as it pleased him.

[19] How could a body be a body with only one part? [20] But the numerous parts form only one body. [21] The eye cannot

[71

declare its independence from the hand because it is different, nor the head from the feet. [22] Not at all! In fact, the parts which seem unimportant are essential. [23] To those parts of our body which are less acceptable we give greater acceptance, and those which seem unattractive we adorn [24] because our attractive parts don't need it. God has so constructed the body that greater honor should be given to the parts which seem inferior, so that the [25] body will not split over "who's who" but truly experience mutual caring. [26] When one part experiences pain, all hurt with it; and when one is honored all share in the celebration.

[27] You all are the Body of Christ and each of you is a special part. [28] Just remember, God has placed different parts in this Body called the Church and has given them their function. First, there are the special messengers, then the witnesses, then teachers; after them are those who do miraculous acts, those who have a special gift for healing, those who are assistants and administrators and speakers in various ecstatic utterances. [29] Are all special messengers? Or witnesses? Are all teachers or miracle workers? [30] Are all endowed with healing powers? Do all speak in ecstasy? Do all interpret their ecstatic speech? [31] You should eagerly desire the more important gifts, yet I must stress to you the greatest gift of all—love!

Love is the greatest of God's gifts

13 [1] Love makes all other gifts appear as nothing. For example, if I speak with the eloquence of earth and the ecstasy of heaven and yet express myself without love, my words are superficial like the brazen sound of a gong or the clash of a cymbal. [2] If I have a gift which enables me to witness to God's truth, or to understand all God's hidden secrets and have knowledge of everything, and if I have the kind of trust that removes mountains, and do not have love, then I am a phony. [3] Neither do I get anywhere just by giving my wealth

to feed the poor—not even by sacrificing my life for what I believe. Without love, even these sacrifices don't count.
[4] Let me describe love. Love stays in difficult relationships with kindness. Love does not play "one-up-man-ship," nor does it react to those who do. [5] Love is not rude or grasping or overly sensitive, nor does love search for imperfections and faults in others. [6] Love celebrates what is real, not what is perverse or incomplete. [7] Love is the most enduring quality of human existence. It keeps on keeping on; it trusts in God in every situation and expects God to act in all circumstances. Nothing can destroy love.

[8] Compare love's endurance with all the other functions or gifts. Proclamations will fade away eventually, tongues will stop speaking, knowledge will have no meaning when everyone knows everything. [9] In our present form of existence, our knowledge is partial and incomplete just like our preaching; [10] but when the fulfillment appears, that is the end of the fragmented.

[11] For instance, when I was a child, it was quite proper for me to think and speak and act like a child; but when I became an adult, I stopped functioning like a child. [12] In our present condition it is like looking through a smoke-stained glass, but one day we will see face to face. At present my knowledge is still fragmented, but then I shall know reality as fully as God knows me now. [13] Today we experience trust, expectation, and love, as realities, but love is by far the greatest. [14:1] So above all else, set your desire on love.

On speaking ecstatically

14 [1b] It is good also to want spiritual gifts but especially to communicate the good news. [2] Compare this gift with making ecstatic utterances. When a person speaks ecstatically, only God knows what he is saying; he speaks things which remain secret to the people around him. [3] But when a person really communicates God's message intelligibly, those who hear are strengthened, encouraged, and affirmed. ⁴ The one gift strengthens the speaker while the other strengthens the whole fellowship. ⁵ I wish each of you could experience ecstatic speaking, but I had rather have you give witness to the good news. Witnessing to the good news is more effective than ecstatic speaking unless someone translates the sounds so that the whole fellowship may be strengthened.

⁶ My friends, what effect will I have on you if I speak unintelligible sounds in ecstasy? My ecstatic speech will not help you unless I bring a clear revelation from God or share my knowledge or express the good news or give some teaching. ⁷ No meaning can be derived from unintelligible sounds. Take musical instruments as an example; unless the wind instruments or stringed instruments give distinct sounds, no one will understand their message. ⁸ If the trumpet gives an unclear sound, what soldier will interpret it as a command to attack the enemy? ⁹ Don't you see that unless you speak clearly and distinctly, you will not get your message across—you will only be talking into the air.

¹⁰ Or take language as another example. There are numerous languages in the world and each has meaning to those who speak it. ¹¹ If, however, I don't understand a person's language, I will be a foreigner to him and he will be a foreigner to me. ¹² You have a strong desire for spiritual endowments, and I urge you to excel in them—in order that you may strengthen the fellowship. ¹³ In other words, let the person speaking in an unknown language pray that he may interpret the message clearly.

¹⁴ Prayer in ecstatic speech is prayer in the Spirit, but my mind is not active in it. ¹⁵ So here is my own decision concerning using special endowments. I will address God in the Spirit, but I will understand what I am saying. I will sing in the Spirit, but I will understand the words I am singing. ¹⁶ If you don't connect the Spirit's activity in your emotions with your mind, how can others participate in the worship? If, for ex-

ample, you are giving thanks in the Spirit, how can the uninformed know when to say "amen"? [17] You may truly be offering thanks, but the others cannot be strengthened if they don't know what you're saying. [18] I thank God that I speak in ecstasy more than any of you, [19] but in a Christian gathering I had rather speak five words everyone understands than ten thousand that they don't.

[20] My friends, don't be like children in understanding. In doing evil it's OK to be like children (quickly forget it); but in understanding be adult. [21] In the record the Lord says, "I will speak to my people through a nation with a different language. And even then they will not hear me." [22] So speaking in ecstasy is a demonstration for those on the outside, not the insiders. And the clear communication of the good news is needed by those already in the fellowship. [23] If your entire group is assembled with everyone speaking in ecstasy and an outsider comes in, it will be a sign for him, all right—a sign you are crazy. [24] But if the same person attends your group meeting and each of you shares experiences of how the good news is affecting his or her life, he will identify with what you say and will be convinced of his needs. [25] With this clear communication of the truth about himself he will bow his head, open his heart and receive the presence of God into his life.

Guidelines for your group meetings

[26] So, my friends, when your group meets, let each person participate. One may have a song to sing, another an insight to share, another a prayer, another a special truth, and still another its application. Combine these acts of worship to strengthen the fellowship. [27] If you have persons who must speak their message in ecstasy, don't have more than two or three per meeting, and let them speak one at a time. Then have someone in the group translate their sounds into meaning. [28] If there is no translator present, don't have ecstatic messages—let the one so disposed speak to himself and to God. [29] Have

[75

two or three witness the good news in their lives while the others compare their experiences to that of the witnesses. [30] If while one is sharing, another person in the fellowship receives a special insight, let the first witness defer to him. [31] Each person should have an opportunity to share so that the whole group can learn and be encouraged from each member. [32] In these worship experiences each person should have control over his own spirit. [33] God does not create confusion but harmony and understanding in both your group and all the others.

[34] Since much of the confusion in your particular group arises from the women, I suggest that for the present they keep quiet in the group meetings. [35] If they have questions, let them inquire of their husbands at home. Their constant interruptions in your group meetings have been most discourteous.

[36] Tell me this, has God's message been transmitted through you or have you been receivers only? [37] If any member of your group considers himself to be a communicator of the good news or to have special insight, then let him recognize that this message I am writing is special and from the Lord. [38] If any group member is insensitive to this fact, don't bother with trying to convince him. [39] Finally, my friends, eagerly desire to communicate good news and don't forbid speaking in ecstasy. [40] Whatever you do in your group meetings, be courteous and maintain orderliness.

The resurrection of Christ

15 [1] My friends, I am reaffirming the good news which I have already proclaimed to you. You received it and placed your confidence in it, [2] and you are being made whole by its power if you are faithful to what I taught you, unless you have been playing a game.

[3] I proclaimed to you from the first the good news which I myself received:

Christ died for us as forecast in the record.

⁴ He was buried. He arose from death on the third day as the record predicted.

⁵ And he was seen by Peter, then by his twelve special messengers. ⁶ He also was seen by more than five hundred Christians at one time, most of whom are alive at the time of my writing, though some have died. ⁷ Later he was seen by James and again by all the special messengers. ⁸ Finally I, a late arrival, saw him face to face; ⁹ and I feel unworthy to be called a special messenger because I tried to destroy the entire Christian community. ¹⁰ Whoever I am today is the result of God's unconditional love for me. And his love for me did not go without my positive response. I have worked harder and more diligently than all the others. Yet it was not I who was working but God, giving me the gift of his unconditional love. ¹¹ It is immaterial whether they or I proclaimed the good news to you; you have received it.

Belief in the resurrection is basic to the faith

¹² You were told by both them and me that Christ arose from the dead. So how can some of you say, "There is no resurrection"? ¹³ If resurrection is not a reality, then Christ's resurrection is an illusion, ¹⁴ our proclamation a waste of time, and your faith a fantasy. ¹⁵ And besides this, we are liars because we have taken the witness stand declaring that God raised Christ from death. Obviously, God did not raise Christ if the dead do not rise. ¹⁶ And if the dead do not rise, Christ's resurrection, I repeat, is an illusion. ¹⁷ And if Christ has not been raised, your faith is a fantasy and you are still estranged from God. ¹⁸ Further, those who have already died have lost their being. ¹⁹ If our expectation of Christ is limited to this life, then we deserve sympathy more than anyone else.

²⁰ But Christ *has* arisen from death; in fact, he is the first to enter death and come back. ²¹ As death entered existence by a man, so resurrection has come through a man. ²² Just as the

human race died in Adam, so the race will be made alive in Christer. [23] Each person will be made alive in proper sequence. Christ has led the way. Next in line will be his people at his final coming. [24] Then will come the climax of history when Christ will hand over the kingdom to the Father. Before this ultimate consummation, Christ must overthrow every alien authority, government, and power. [25] Christ must remain in control until every enemy becomes a willing subject. [26] The last enemy to submit will be death.

[27] According to the record, God has given Christ authority over the created world. Obviously, this does not mean God has placed himself under Christ. [28] When Christ has subdued the warring elements in creation, he will place himself under God's control so that God may be everything to everyone in every situation.

[29] If the dead do not rise, what do you have to say about those who are baptized for the dead? If there is no resurrection, why are they baptized for the dead?

[30] If there is no resurrection, why do I risk my life every hour of the day? [31] Personally, I face death every day. That fact is as certain as my pride in your growth in the Lord. [32] Tell me, why did I fight those men at Ephesus—men who fought like tigers—if I have hope in this life only? If resurrection is an illusion, let us all join the crowd that says, "Eat, drink, and have a good time because soon we will all be dead." [33] Do not buy that illusion. If you believe that nonsense, your behavior will soon show it. [34] Be alert to the right way and don't keep wandering off the track. Some have copied your behavior who do not know God—and that's a shame.

What "resurrection" means

[35] Some of you will ask, "What is the nature of resurrection? In what type of body are people raised?" [36] You do understand that death is a part of life, don't you? Unless a seed dies, it does not sprout life. [37] When you plant a seed, whether of

wheat or corn, it doesn't look anything like the plant that comes from it. [38] When it sprouts and grows, it develops a form in keeping with the Creator's purpose—the seed has its form and the plant its form. [39] Not all bodies are alike. Humans have one kind of flesh, animals another, birds another, and fish still another. [40] In similar fashion there are earthly bodies and heavenly bodies. [41] The splendor of the earthly body is one thing, but the splendor of the heavenly is another. For example, the sun has its brilliance, the moon its light, and the stars their light. Each star differs in its brilliance.

[42] Each of these illustrations points clearly to the meaning of the resurrection. The body which dies is like the seed sown. The body which is raised imperishable is like the plant. [43] It is sown in fragments, it is raised in wholeness; it is sown with limitations, it is raised beyond boundaries. [44] It is planted a physical body, it is raised a spiritual body. There is indeed a physical body and a spiritual body. [45] The record states that like the two bodies there are two Adams—the first a living person, the second a life-giving spirit.

[46] You will note that the physical preceded the spiritual and not the other way around. [47] The first human representative originated from the earth; the second representative was the Lord originating in heaven. [48] Whatever the first human was, so are all other human beings; and, as the Lord is, so are those who are related to him. [49] As we have shared the physical form of humanity, we will share the spiritual form of Christ.

Christ's resurrection has conquered death

[50] I want to be very clear with you. Humans in their physical form do not enter directly into their future life any more than a constantly changing thing becomes changeless. [51] But I will reveal a secret to you. Not all of us will sleep in death, but we will all be transformed—[52] in a flash; in the flick of an eye; at the signal. The signal will sound and the dead will experience resurrection, [53] a real transformation because my constantly

[79

changing person will acquire permanence and my person which is subject to death will receive life eternal. [54] When I as a constantly changing person acquire permanence and as a dying person receive life forever, at that moment as the record states, "death will be conquered and life will reign." [55] So I confidently ask, "Now, death, where is your threat? Grave, where is your conquest?" [56] The threat death holds is a consequence of our estrangement from God, and the rules reveal and accentuate it. [57] But I thank God who enables us to conquer death and estrangement through Jesus Christ our Lord.

[58] So, my dear friends, do not be shaken in your faith by the threat of death. Hold steady, don't let anything throw you. Keep doing the Lord's work because you are aware of its worth now and your reward in the future.

Concluding instructions

16 [1] I have just a word about the offering for the fellowship of Christpersons; I want you to function like the churches in Galatia. [2] When your group meets on the first day of the week, I want each of you to contribute a portion of your earnings so there need be no collection when I arrive. [3] On my arrival, I will send your collection by the persons to whom you give letters of approval to assist the poor Christpersons in Jerusalem. [4] If you think it best for me to go, they will accompany me.

[5] I will visit you after I go through Macedonia. I do pass near you on that trip. [6] I may even decide to stay with you and perhaps spend the winter with you, and you can assist me with my further travels. [7] My present plan does not call for a visit with you, but I am looking forward to being with you later, if that fits into God's plan. [8] I now plan to remain in Ephesus until Pentecost. [9] Here I am experiencing a great opportunity, and I am quite effective in spite of the strong opposition I have encountered.

[10] If Timothy comes to visit with you, be sure that he re-

ceives a warm welcome so he will not be anxious. He is doing God's work just as I do. ¹¹ Don't reject this brother; rather, accept him and send him along to me because I expect him to accompany your delegates. ¹² With regard to Apollos, I wanted him to accompany the brothers who are delivering this letter, but that was not what he wanted. He will be coming when he has an opportunity.

¹³ Keep your awareness sharp. Be steady in your trust. Function like adults. Be strong. ¹⁴ Do everything with a loving attitude. ¹⁵ Take Stephanas's family as your model. They were the first Christians in your area, and they have always been responsive to the ministry. ¹⁶ I request you, my friends, to respect all the workers of the Lord who come your way and be responsive to them.

¹⁷ I rejoice at the arrival of Stephanas, Fortunatus, and Achaicus because they gave me the support from your group which was lacking because you weren't here with me. ¹⁸ They have encouraged me a great deal and their report back to you will be equally encouraging, so welcome their return.

¹⁹ The churches here in Asia Minor send you a warm greeting. A special greeting also comes from Aquila and Priscilla and from the members of their house church.

²⁰ Your brothers and sisters send greetings. When you meet, embrace each other with an affectionate hug.

²¹ Look, I am signing this letter with my own hand.

²² If any person does not love our Lord Jesus Christ, let him be an outcast—and may the Lord soon come!

²³ May the unconditional love of our Lord Jesus Christ be with you.

²⁴ And I want each of you to know that I love you in Christ.

Second Corinthians

INTRODUCTION

Before he wrote 1 Corinthians, Paul sent Timothy to Corinth to check on the situation there. Timothy was present when the letter arrived and saw that it did not completely fulfill its purpose of quelling disharmony in the church. (See introduction for 1 Corinthians.) When Timothy reported this to Paul, the apostle decided to make a quick trip to Corinth, only to find that his presence caused more problems than it solved. (This is the "painful visit" referred to in 2:1.)

Upon his return to Ephesus, he wrote what is called the "severe letter" to Corinth, a biting, sarcastic letter containing a stirring defense of himself and a severe reprimand for the hostile and divisive Corinthians. It has not been preserved in its entirety, but most scholars agree that chapters 10–13 of 2 Corinthians came from this "severe letter." Paul sends this letter to Corinth by Titus, and then, with a heavy heart, leaves Ephesus for Macedonia.

In Macedonia Titus rejoins Paul to tell him that the crisis has passed in Corinth and the situation is under control. Paul then joyfully writes what we know as 2 Corinthians (chapters 1–9), and dispatches Titus back to Corinth with the letter. A suggested date for the writing is about 56 or 57 A.D.

Admittedly, this is a theory, but it is a theory with a strong basis for validity. Even the casual reader cannot help noticing the abrupt change of mood and thought in chapters 10–13, as contrasted with 1–9.

Also, chapter 6:14–7:1 seems out of place and is thought to be part of the "previous letter" which Paul refers to in 1 Corinthians 5:9.

SECOND CORINTHIANS

1 ¹ This letter is from Paul, a special messenger of Christ in accordance with God's purpose, and Timothy, along with your fellow Christians here in Achaia who join me in sending this letter to you at Corinth. ² May unconditional love be yours from God who is our Father and from Jesus Christ, the Lord of our life.

Encouragement for times of suffering

³ May God, who is the Father of our Lord Jesus Christ and is the source of compassion and unlimited encouragement, be fulfilled through the joyous response of his people. ⁴ He encourages us in our suffering so that we can share our experience of his encouragement with those who have similar needs. ⁵ The more we know suffering with Christ, the greater our share of Christ's encouragement. ⁶ I interpret my experiences in the light of how they can help you, and this perspective gives me endurance. When I suffer, this will bring encouragement and wholeness to you. My being encouraged will also encourage you. ⁷ My confidence in your outcome is unshaken—as you have shared the suffering, you will share the encouragement.

⁸ We want you to be aware of the difficulty we experienced in the province of Asia. Our stress was so great that we felt we could snap at any time; actually, it would have been easier to die. ⁹ It was as though we were under a death sentence and had no power to overturn it. ¹⁰ Having reached our limits and beyond, we could only trust in God. And God freed us to live, he continues to free us, and we believe he will free us in the future. ¹¹ Through your many prayers and gifts you also are participating in our ministry, and a host of persons will give thanks for your prayers for us.

Straight communication from Paul

[12] I claim with pride that I have lived my life in the world with complete openness and straightforwardness—not with sophisticated intellectualizing but by the power of God's unconditional love. And, if possible, I have been even more open with you. I feel really straight with myself when I make such an affirmation. [13] So now I want to write only what you can read and understand, and I hope you will finally understand me completely [14] just as you partially understand me now. I want you to be proud of me just as I shall be proud of you on history's final day.

[15] Because I was confident of this, I intended to come to you earlier to give you the pleasure of two visits. [16] I thought of visiting you on my journey to Macedonia and then of visiting you again. Possibly you would have shared my expenses for the return trip to Judea. [17] When I tell you that I considered this possibility, do you think I am being frivolous? Do you think I am wishy-washy, saying yes one moment and no the next? [18] Just as God's communication has no double meaning, neither has mine. [19] When Silvanus and Timothy and I presented God's trustworthy communication through his Son Jesus Christ to you, we did not do so ambivalently. [20] Each of us affirmed that Jesus is God's yes to life. Every promise God has made to us finds its fulfillment in Christ. He is God's consummate yes to existence and the key to God's ultimate fulfillment through us.

[21] And it is this God who has securely united us together in Christ—both you and us—and has given us his gifts. [22] He has stamped his approval on us and given us the Spirit as his pledge to us. [23] I call on him now to testify against me if I am lying. He knows why I have not come to Corinth—I wanted to spare you. [24] Whether I visit or not, I am not responsible for your choices about your faith, but I can help you live more effectively and experience more joy. Your steadfastness in the faith is your own responsibility.

Forgiving the offender

2 [1] I have made a firm decision not to make another painful visit to you. [2] For if I make you sad, then who is left to cheer me up except the one in whom I have caused pain? [3] I wrote you the other letter before my visit to admonish you, hoping to avoid being depressed by the problems you have. I need your encouragement, and I am confident that you all want me to have joy.

[4] When I wrote the first letter to you, I was very disappointed in you, so much so that I actually wept. I didn't write to depress or discourage you, but to show my love and concern for you. [5] If any member has grieved you, it has not affected my attitude toward you. Well, I suppose it has affected me to some degree because I do not want to place anyone under more pressure than he can endure. [6] I believe your united rejection of the offender has been sufficient punishment. [7] You should now reverse your actions. Forgive him and reach out to him; accept him; encourage him before he is overwhelmed with rejection. [8] In both word and deed tell him that you love him. [9] I actually wrote you to exclude this fellow to see if you would be obedient to my leadership in every detail. [10] If you forgive this person, I forgive him and if I forgive him for your sake, it is equivalent to Christ's forgiving him. [11] We offer this forgiveness so that our Adversary will not get an illegal grip on any of us; we know how he works.

[12] When I came to Troas to proclaim Christ's good news, I found a high level of receptivity from the people, [13] but I had a great deal of anxiety because Titus, my brother, was not there. So, I left for Macedonia.

Worthwhileness in ourselves and others

[14] That just reminds me how utterly grateful I am to God who enables us through Christ to feel worthwhile as persons in situations that call our worth into question—and in the process he spreads the perfume of his presence into otherwise odious

circumstances. [15] Our responses to life have the effect of a God-scented perfume both to those who are being made whole and to those who are disintegrating. [16] To the latter we have the smell of death, but to the former we smell like life itself. Who can shoulder such responsibility? [17] My co-workers and I do not dilute God's message. With genuine openness, because we are sent by God and speak in his presence, we communicate the Christ-message.

3 [1] My friends, must we struggle over our relationship? Must I recommend myself? Do I need, as others do, letters of recommendation written to you or letters of recommendation from you? [2] You constitute my letter of recommendation, observable to everybody who knows me, because it is written in your hearts. [3] Your lives are my letter of recommendation to you from Christ delivered to you by us. As a letter you were written not with pen and ink but through the agency of God's Spirit, not on stones, as God wrote before, but on the tender, sensitive stuff of your inner being.

Living by the Spirit rather than rules

[4] It is because of Christ that I can trust God to recommend me. [5] When I accept his recommendation in this fashion, it does not mean that I am self-sufficient and able to stand on my performance alone; rather, God is the source of my sufficiency. [6] God has also enabled us to communicate his new contract with you, which is not formulated in a new set of rules but is established in the Spirit. Rules kill, but the Spirit gives life. [7] Compare the giving of the rules with reception of the Spirit. The presentation of the rules which result in death was so brilliant that the Israelites could not look directly upon Moses' face because of the glare of the presence of God—and the rules he received were destined to pass away. [8] Won't the gift of the Spirit be more luminous? [9] If the gift of rules which condemn a person was deemed marvelous, isn't the gift of a

right relationship a greater marvel? [10] As marvelous as receiving the rules may have been, this gift is fading away because it is superseded by the reception of the Spirit. [11] If what is abolished is marvelous, how much more marvelous is that which remains.

The Spirit sets persons free

[12] Because I am confident that this is so, I can speak openly to you. [13] I am not communicating with you as Moses did when he veiled his face so that the Israelites could not perceive the final destiny of the rules. [14] They were blind then and they are still blind when they read the account of the old covenant. Its meaning is veiled to them, but Christ has unveiled it for us. [15] Unfortunately, even today when they read the rules given through Moses, their perception is veiled.

[16] But when anyone turns to Christ, the veil is removed, just as when Moses spoke to God the veil came off. [17] This is God's Spirit at work and wherever the Spirit of God operates, he sets persons free. [18] With the veil lifted from our eyes we see the ultimate purpose of God reflected in Christ, and as we keep this vision before us we are continually transformed by it. We move from one area of fulfillment to another as the Spirit acts upon us.

The inner light Christ gives us

4 [1] Since I have the task of enabling persons to change, I do not become discouraged as long as I receive God's mercy. [2] To be effective, I have rejected game-playing, and a manipulative lifestyle. Neither do I force God's message to accommodate things as they are. But by living in harmony with Christ within and what I know of God's purpose, I reflect reality to each person and to God himself.

[3] If some do not perceive the good news, it is those who have not opened themselves to reality. [4] These persons have become insensitive because of their choices to fulfill themselves through

the worship of the temporal creations of this age. So they do not perceive the image of the eternal God who is represented in Christ. [5] Not I, but Jesus Christ our Lord, originated this good news. And because of what he has done in my life, I am your servant.

[6] God, who originally caused the first light of creation to shine in the darkness, through Christ has caused the light of reality to shine in the depths of our being to give us an awareness of his own person. [7] But we carry this inner light like a treasure in a breakable pot to evidence the fact that the tremendous energy which it releases comes from God and not from our own achievement. [8] We are quite human. We experience every kind of pressure but we are not confined; we are often confused but never totally immobilized. [9] Persecuted by men, we are not abandoned by God. Thrown to the ground by our opponents, we are not totally wiped out. [10] These negative experiences remind me that I am daily sharing the death of Christ while the inner resources which these experiences call forth manifest my participation in the resurrection. [11] During our life we constantly experience different kinds of death for Jesus' sake so that new dimensions of the life he revealed may be expressed through us. [12] Our experience of death produces your experience of life.

Ultimate fulfillment through unconditional love

[13] We have the same attitude of faith possessed by one of our past leaders who said, "I believe and so I declare it." We also believe and state what that means to us. [14] Just as God raised Jesus from death, he will also raise us with Jesus along with you. [15] So I view our entire experience as for your sake, so that as you give thanks for God's unconditional love it may ring like a great chorus cheering for God's ultimate fulfillment.

[16] No, we don't grow weary and discouraged. While physically we change daily, our spiritual power is renewed day after

day. [17] Our minor pain, which is temporary, prepares us to experience a far greater degree of ultimate fulfillment. [18] During our temporary life here, we don't fix our gaze on the physical world but rather on its invisible source; the things we can see with our eyes are passing away, but the essence of things which we sense with our hearts lasts forever.

5 [1] We are confident, then, that when the earthly house of our body perishes, we have another dwelling to move into, one not of human construction, but imperishable in the presence of God. [2] Some of our present circumstances cause us to groan with a deep desire to move into our imperishable house. [3] When we make this transition, we will not be a naked spirit without a body. [4] Even though we struggle with both pain and human limitation while we are living in our earthly body, we don't want merely to be stripped of our body but we long, rather, to be clothed with another, so that our human possibilities may be actualized in all their fullness. [5] This is no empty hope, because God created us for this very purpose, and he gave us his Spirit as a pledge that he will ultimately fulfill our deepest longings.

The love of Christ motivates us

[6] But while we are living in our human body, we do not have face-to-face contact with the Lord. [7] We live by trusting him rather than actually seeing him. [8] Our confidence in our continued life with him is so strong that we would actually prefer to move out of our physical bodies into face-to-face contact with him. [9] For that reason, we live the kind of life that, whether we are in his immediate presence or experience it through faith, we may have his acceptance.

[10] For the time of final evaluation is coming, when each of us must appear before Christ to be evaluated for the kind of life he has lived, that is, whether it has been productive or not.

[11] Because of the horror of living an unproductive, meaningless life which denies God, we urge every person to fulfill his destiny before God. Our motivation is evident to the Lord, and I hope it is to you also.

[12] We are not recommending our ministry again; rather, we are giving you information that will enable you to defend us to those who pride themselves on appearance and not true motivation. [13] If we are standing outside ourselves in ecstasy, it is for God; if we are just being normal, it is for your sake. [14] But in every case Christ's love motivates and rules us because we recognize that he died for everyone, and therefore all persons died with him. [15] But he died—he has given his life for all of us —so that all persons may come alive and live through him, fulfilling our true self but not the false one.

The transforming message of reconciliation

[16] From this time on, then, let us look at others not with our limited human insight. Although we have perceived Christ humanly, let us no longer look at him that way. [17] Because if any person has been joined with Christ in this new relationship of death and life, he or she is a new person; the old way of looking at life has passed away, and from this new perspective everything has become fresh and new.

[18] This new life and new perspective comes from God who has brought us back to himself in Jesus Christ and then has given us the task of announcing that all things have been put right between us and him. [19] You see, God was acting in Christ to make the relationship between all creation and himself a harmonious one by not counting persons guilty who have gotten off the track. [20] And he has entrusted to us this message that all is now right between everyone and himself. So now we are ambassadors for Christ; it is as if God were speaking directly to you through our lips. In Christ's behalf we urge you to accept for yourselves God's reconciling act. [21] For Christ, who never broke his relationship to God, did for our sake ex-

perience brokenness and emptiness so that our brokenness could be transformed into participation in the life of God.

Acting as God's agents

6 [1] Because then, we work together with God, we urge you not to receive God's unconditional love uselessly. [2] (Incidentally, God says, "I have responded to you at the appropriate time; I have assisted you since the day you began to find wholeness." Be certain this is the time of response; today is the day for wholeness.)

[3] When we work with God we don't block any person's access to him so that our ministry can't be criticized. [4] In all our experiences we choose to act in a manner that demonstrates that we are truly God's agents. For example, we can endure with patience and fortitude an enormous amount of suffering, of material needs, of emotional stress, [5] even beatings, imprisonment, riots, and numerous tasks performed through sleepless nights and foodless days. [6] We show that we are truly agents of God by the purity of our conscious intentions, by gaining more knowledge, by patient waiting, by kindness, by responding to the Holy Spirit, by having sincere love, [7] by the truths which we express, by the power of God we demonstrate, by using all the resources which are available through our right relation with God.

[8] We maintain our integrity in the midst of conflicting reports that we are honorable and dishonorable, reports that we are evil and good; they say we are shysters, but we are genuine. [9] Some persons do not know us at all, but God knows us very well; frequently at the edge of death, we are nevertheless quite alive. We suffer a great deal, but obviously hardship has not killed us. [10] As God's agents we experience a lot of disappointment, but we can always find something to celebrate. We don't own anything, but we are enriching the lives of many persons. It may appear that we have nothing, but really we have everything.

[93

Right relationships for Christpersons

[11] My friends at Corinth! I have told you how it is with me; I have described all my feelings; I am really open to you in love. [12] If there is still a block in our relation, it is not in me. There may be one in you. [13] If you still have negative feelings toward me (I know I'm speaking as an authoritative parent), be generous, forgive me, and open yourself wide to me.

[14] My dear friends, please don't enter into binding contracts (like marriage) with non-Christians. How can that work for you? Do people in a right relationship with God have the same goals as those who have not made this crucial choice? Can there be a lasting relationship between those who live in sensitive awareness and those who are insensitive? [15] What connection is there between Christ and the devil? Or, what does someone who trusts Christ have in common with someone who doesn't trust? [16a] The question boils down to this: How can Christpersons have harmonious relationships with those who are not Christpersons?

[16b] You can't. For you are the house of God himself. He has told us what this means: "I will live in them and express myself through them; I will be the source of all their needs and they will find their fulfillment through me. [17] So get yourself untangled from destructive relationships and establish wholesome relations. [18] Discover for yourself that I will be like a father to you and you will be like a son or a daughter to me. That is what I have promised."

7 [1] Because God has promised to be our Father and to relate intimately to us, let us change our destructive behavior and our damaging perception of ourselves and out of reverence for God aim at being whole persons with each decision we make.

Paul: "How it is with me"

[2] Again, I urge you to open yourselves to our ministry. We have taken advantage of nobody, we have destroyed nobody,

we have cheated nobody. [3] I have no desire to discount you because you are part of my life whether I am under the threat of death or celebrating life. [4] Nor do I hesitate to tell you how it is with me—I am full of pride because of you. The knowledge of your relationship with God gives me courage and joy even in the midst of pressures and troubles.

[5] Even after we arrived in Macedonia, we had no peace because we were pressured on every side. On the outside we were threatened by riots and attacks; on the inside we were plagued by all kinds of fear. [6] But in spite of our feelings and circumstances God, who encourages the depressed, encouraged us by a visit from Titus. [7] My encouragement came not only from my relationship with Titus personally, but also from the fact that you had been such a source of encouragement to him. He went on to tell me how much you care for me, how you have wept over my situation, and how deep is your concern for me, which gives me more cause for joy.

Productive grief

[8] Although I grieved you with my previous letter, I do not alter my instructions. For a time I considered changing my mind but not any longer. My directive caused you grief for a while, but now that is over. [9] Today I really celebrate, not because I grieved you but because your grief caused you to change and has drawn you closer to God; your pain did not make you losers. [10] In fact, grief which helps you change toward wholeness is godly and is not to be regretted. But grief which is nothing but self-pity is destructive and should be abandoned. [11] Again, evaluate the kind of grief which you experienced. Look at what it has produced in you: you have become more eager to relate to other persons; you have gotten rid of your masks; you have had appropriate anger; you have reverence and respect; you have experienced a deep uniting of your emotions; you have been more eager to serve God than ever before; you have learned about justice. You have taken

[95

the appropriate action in the troublesome matter of which I wrote to you. [12] When I wrote the hard letter to you, I was not primarily concerned with the one who had done the wrong nor with the one who had suffered the wrong, but with your concern for us. I wanted both you and God to know my concern for you. [13] So, for all these reasons I was encouraged. And to add to my encouragement we all had our joy ignited with the joy Titus was experiencing, because his spirit was truly set at rest through his visit with you.

[14] I do not regret a single boast I have made concerning you. Just as I was straight in my reprimand of you, I was accurate in my bragging to Titus about you. [15] And Titus's affection for you is very deep as he recalls how you were obedient to my injunction to receive him, even though you did it with anxiety and hesitation. [16] I do celebrate the fact that in all your affairs my confidence has been restored in you.

Guidance on giving

8 [1] Furthermore, my friends, I want to inform you about the measure of God's unconditional love which he demonstrated to the churches in Macedonia. [2] In the midst of their suffering, their deep joy and their poverty inspired them to give liberally to others. [3] I witness to the fact that according to their ability—yes, even beyond their ability—they gave of their own free will. [4] They literally begged us to take their money and take responsibility for distributing it to Christpersons in need. [5] And contrary to our expectations they had their giving in the proper priority. First, they gave themselves to God and then contributed to us according to his will.

[6] Now I had urged Titus, who had begun teaching you how to give, to help you mature in giving. [7] Just as you have abounded in all the gifts like faith, the power to speak, knowledge, your love for us, and in deep desire, I hope you will also abound in giving.

[8] What I have to say is not a direct commandment, but I am

motivated by the eagerness of others' gifts when I urge you to demonstrate the sincerity of your love through your giving. [9] You know the unconditional love of our Lord Jesus Christ; he had all the wealth of God and he became a pauper so that through his poverty we could become wealthy. [10] Here now is my advice. About a year ago you were eager to make an offering, but you never finished making it. It is now time for you to complete it. [11] You must match your inner willingness with your outward behavior by completing it according to what you have. [12] If you have a desire to give, your desire is acceptable to me when you give according to your ability. (Certainly, you can't give what you don't have.)

[13] My intention is not to ease the load of another group of Christians by overloading you. [14] I want equality among God's people. At the present you have an abundance and others are in need—so give to them. In the future when they are prospering, you may be in need and they will give to you. This mutual sharing of abundance will equal things out. [15] You recall the saying, "The man who harvested a bumper crop had nothing left over, and the one who had a short crop lacked nothing."

Our brother Titus

[16] I am grateful to God that he inspired Titus to care for you as much as I do. [17] When I first asked him to visit you, he was willing; but more important, he really wanted to visit you. [18] With Titus I have sent a brother who is highly esteemed in all the churches as Christ's person. [19] In addition, he has selected another person to travel with us to observe how carefully we distribute the gifts we have received from generous contributors. [20] By his observing how we share these gifts, we avoid any accusation of partiality or unfairness. [21] Our intentions are pure; we are totally open to both the Lord's inspection and man's. [22] And, we have sent along another Christian brother who has been tested for his zealous dedication in many phases of ministry. He is most eager to accompany Titus be-

[97

cause of his confidence in your desire to make your contributions. [23] If you want to know about Titus's status in working for you, he is my partner and my co-worker. About our traveling companions—they bring greetings from the churches here and manifest Christ himself to you. [24] I urge you in all the congregations to show genuine love to these Christpersons. Prove to them that my bragging was not false.

Give generously in response to God's gift to you

9 [1] I do not need to urge you to make a contribution to help take care of some very poor Godpersons. [2] I know how eager you are to make your contribution; in fact, you in Achaia have been prepared for a year, and I've been bragging about your attitude through Macedonia. My reports of your eagerness to give have inspired most of them to contribute. [3] I have, however, sent these companions in the faith to make sure you are prepared, lest all the bragging I have been doing turns into empty words. [4] If perhaps some Macedonian Christpersons come with me on my visit to you, because of my bragging I would certainly be embarrassed and so would you should you be unprepared to make your contribution. [5] So, I have requested these brothers to come to you in advance of my visit and take up the offering. Recall that you promised to give your offering. I want you to give with a generous spirit, not because you have been pressured.

[6] Remember the saying: "A stingy sower will reap a meager harvest, and a generous sower will reap a bumper crop." [7] Each of you must decide in your own heart how much you can give—and give it. Whatever amount you decide to give, give it freely without feeling under pressure, because God loves a cheerful giver. [8] And God is able to express his unconditional love to you in a variety of ways so that you will always have what you need for every good work. [9] (There's another saying which goes like this: "The godly man makes a broad distribu-

tion of his gifts, especially to the poor. His generous action will always be remembered.") [10] May God who created the seed which the farmer plants provide bread for you to eat, cause your efforts to be productive, and enrich all of your relationships. [11] I hope you will be enriched in everything, even a simple desire, thus fulfilling you completely. Those who receive your gifts will be utterly grateful to God for what you have sent by us.

[12] Your gifts to these Godpersons not only meet their needs, but cause many of them to give thanks to God. [13] Furthermore, your gifts will cause them to praise God because you have enacted the good news by this simple sharing of your goods with them and all others. (See what your generous giving to these persons and all others accomplishes!) [14] These Godpersons pray for you and earnestly desire to be related to you because of God's exceptional action in you. [15] Reflecting on your generous gifts causes me to say, "Thanks be to God for his indescribable gift."

Paul pleads for understanding

10 [1] I, whom some of you recognize as Paul, am pleading with you with the humility and tenderness which Christ demonstrated. Some of you say that in person I am cowardly, but at a distance I am courageous. [2] I really do not wish to display my courage when I am with you, the kind of courage which would issue a strong rebuke to some of you who consider my planning and acting that of an ordinary human being. [3] True, we are human, but we do not use human manipulations to achieve our aims. [4] The tools of our trade are not designed for coercion or manipulation; nevertheless, they are effective through God in destroying the defenses behind which people hide. [5] We wipe out our fantasies and every behavior which competes with our loyalty to God, and we take control of our thoughts, testing their validity by the Spirit of Christ. [6] With

[99

the dynamic energy of these tools I am eager to work on all other Godpersons after I have first corrected your blemishes.

⁷ Do you base your decisions on external appearances? If you have decided that you belong to Christ, just consider that I also belong to him. ⁸ If I were to brag even more about the authority which God has given me—an authority to build you up and not to tear you down—I would not be embarrassed. ⁹ I do not wish, however, to frighten you with threatening letters. ¹⁰ I can imagine some of you saying, "His letters are impressive and potent, reflecting his sense of authority; but his personal presence is unimpressive, and as a preacher he's hopeless." ¹¹ If any of you are making such statements, just be assured that my manner and tone in writing indicate precisely how I will be in person.

Paul's standard and concern

¹² I do not want to be identified with or compared to those boastful persons who brag on themselves. In their braggart clique they compare themselves to one another and evaluate each other by their own standards, a procedure lacking integrity. ¹³ I will not boast without a standard, but I will measure my performance by the standard of love which God has set forth, a standard which applies even to you. ¹⁴ I am not stretching the truth when I claim responsibility for your hearing the good news, because I did come and speak to you. ¹⁵ But I'm not bragging about things I haven't done, or claiming credit for what other leaders have accomplished. I do hope that when your trust in God is greater, I will be more important to you.

¹⁶ I desire to proclaim the good news in the regions beyond you so that never again will I be accused of claiming credit for what another person has done. ¹⁷ Actually, all our bragging in what we have accomplished should be bragging in what the Lord has enabled us to do. ¹⁸ It is not the person who com-

mends himself who is truly acclaimed but the one whom the Lord commends.

"Listen to me," says Paul, "not these impostors!"

11 [1] May God give you patience with me in my foolishness; hold steady while I boast. [2] I am genuinely concerned about you with God's own concern. I have gotten you engaged to Christ, and I want you to have your virginity at the marriage ceremony. [3] I am terribly afraid that you will be deceived by the Deceiver just as Eve was in the Garden. Through this cunning deception, the utter simplicity of your relation to Christ would lose its grip on your mind. [4] These deceivers present a pseudo-Jesus, they disseminate a false spirit, they corrupt the good news—and you are so patient with these impostors!

[5] Your attraction to these impostors concerns me. I am not inferior to the most renowned of the representatives of Christ. [6] I may speak crudely, but I know what I am talking about. There is no deceit in my relation to you; I have made a complete and candid disclosure to you. [7] Tell me, was I wrong to proclaim the good news to you without receiving any pay? It appears to me that you have interpreted my generosity as inferiority. [8] I feel disgusted with your attitude when I recall how I took money from other churches so that I could serve you free of charge. [9] And when I was working among you and had needs, I didn't ask you for a cent. My friends from Macedonia brought me money to provide my necessities. I have never taken a cent from you—and I never will.

[10] I know the reality of Christ and how honestly I have proclaimed him. Nobody will stop me from boasting about that. [11] Do you think my boasting indicates an absence of love for you? God knows the truth if you don't. [12] I plan to close the door on those impostors who consider themselves superior to us. If they wish to boast as I do, let them earn their own keep. [13] They are phony messengers, tricky workers masquerading

as messengers of Christ. [14] This is no great wonder because the Adversary himself masquerades as a heavenly messenger. [15] No wonder his representatives participate in his masquerade. Be assured they will eventually be exposed and properly rewarded.

What Paul has been through as Christ's messenger

[16] I repeat my plea: do not think me insane. Even if you do, accept me as insane and let me brag about what I have done. [17] What I am about to say is not commanded by the Lord; rather, as a fool I am giving free rein to my confident bragging. [18] Because other messengers to you have been boastful of their own personal achievements, I will do the same. [19] You seem to accept such insanity since you are so sane and intelligent! [20] You permit these impostors to enslave you, to free-load on you, to destroy your self-worth, to take your money, to deceive you, to attack you physically.

[21] I suppose it is to my shame to admit that I was too weak to relate to you as they do. But now, let me be so foolish as to be as bold with bragging as they are. [22] Are they Hebrews? I am too. Are they Israelites? I, too, am an Israelite. Are they descendants of Abraham? So am I. [23] They claim to be agents of Christ. It's more than a claim with me; I am a messenger of Christ and a more effective one. I realize I'm boasting recklessly, but I have worked harder, been beaten countless times, been jailed frequently, and often faced death. [24] The Jews beat me five times within one lash of the forty-lash limit. [25] Three times I was beaten with sticks, once I was stoned, three times I was shipwrecked, once I spent twenty-four hours drifting in the open sea. [26] I have made innumerable trips and been threatened by storms, by thieves, by fellow Jews, and by non-Jews. I have been in danger in cities, in deserts, on the sea, and often from impostors. [27] I have worked at the task when I was exhausted, in great hardship, during sleepless nights, without food, exposed to cold without enough clothing. [28] In addition to all these painful circumstances, I have been pressured by

my constant anxiety about all the groups of Christpersons I care for. ²⁹ Because I share the weakness of the weak, and I burn with anger when Christpersons are made to stumble.

³⁰ You see, my own bragging does not concern my achievements, but my weaknesses. ³¹ God, the Father of our Lord Jesus Christ, knows I am telling the truth and not lying, and may he always be praised.

³² Oh, yes, I recall how the governor of Damascus tried to capture me with a full regiment. ³³ My friends stuffed me in a basket and let me down through a window beside the wall and I escaped.

More insight into Paul

12 ¹ Although my boasting may not get the response from you I desire, I will continue anyway by relating to you a very significant experience. ² I recall about fourteen years ago having such an intense experience of Christ that I did not know whether I was in my body or not. It was like being in the immediate presence of God. ³ And I recall (God alone knows whether I was in my body or not) in that state of ecstasy ⁴ hearing ideas which surpass human symbols. ⁵ I can truly boast about that spiritual experience; but for myself I will only brag about my weaknesses.

⁶ I frequently feel an urge to boast; and if I do, I am not a fool because I will be telling the truth. Yet, though I could tell you how it is, I will control myself lest I project a false image of myself. ⁷ And, to keep me from building my self-worth on the number of ecstatic experiences I have had, the Adversary gave me a physical impediment and it helps me keep a sane estimate of myself. ⁸ I prayed earnestly about that impediment; in fact, three times I asked the Lord to remove it. ⁹ And he replied to me: "My unconditional love for you will sustain you. My strength in you comes to full maturity when you are most subject to your weakness." So I will celebrate my physical weaknesses and rely more deeply on the energy of Christ. ¹⁰ I

[103

choose to have a positive attitude toward life in spite of my weaknesses, or those who insult me, or my unmet needs, or my persecutions, or the stress which I experience for Christ's sake. Each time I feel weak, I am made aware of my source of energy.

[11] I probably appear quite ridiculous to you because of my bragging. I was forced into it by your attitudes. You should have bragged about my work because I am in no way inferior to the best representatives of Christ, even though I don't count for anything with you. [12] Obviously, I have been proved a special representative to you with patience, unexplainable deeds, and some powerful healings. [13] And you were inferior to no church except in your financial support of me. (I hope you will forgive me for the error I committed in not demanding support.)

Paul's impending visit

[14] I am preparing to visit you a third time and I will not accept support from you this time, either. I want you to know clearly that I don't want your money but you. Parents take care of children, not the reverse. [15] I am willing to spend all I have, even my own self, for you; yet it appears the more I love you, the less I am loved.

[16] Be that as it may, you say that even though I didn't take anything from you, I was cunning and tricked you. [17] Do you really think I made a profit on you through my associates that I sent to you? [18] I sent Titus and a brother to you. Did either take a cent of support? They both paid their own way just as I did.

[19] Does it appear to you that I am being defensive? I am telling you the truth before God and Christ when I say that all my explanations are meant to build you up. [20] I am quite anxious about our meeting. I am afraid you will not measure up to my expectations, and if you don't, I certainly won't

measure up to yours, either. When I arrive, don't let me find you arguing, jealous of each other, throwing temper tantrums, being selfishly ambitious, slandering others or whispering behind their backs, inflated with pride, or stirring up trouble. ²¹ Clear up this immature behavior so that I will not need to be so hard on you, because I have reports that you are functioning in other immature ways—like sex outside of marriage, and undisciplined pleasure—and have not returned to God's way.

13 ¹ I am preparing for my third visit with you. Our Jewish records maintain that each charge brought against someone should be established by the witness of two or three persons who observed it. (I have met that requirement for confirmation of your behavior.) ² I have previously warned you who are living undisciplined lives, and now I want you to hear me as though I am speaking face to face with you; *I will not let them get by with that behavior if I come again.* ³ And through my severe disciplining of them, you will have the evidence of Christ's power in me. ⁴ It is true that his crucifixion evidences Christ's weakness, but his resurrection evidences the energy of God giving him life. I share his weakness and I also experience the divine energy as I deal with you.

Acceptable behavior for Christpersons

⁵ Take a hard look at your behavior to determine whether Jesus Christ is active among you. You are aware, aren't you, that he is in your midst unless you have closed the door to him? ⁶ I certainly hope you know that we have not excluded him from our lives.

⁷ My prayer to God for you is that you won't close the door on Christ or on significant relationships. I am not seeking personal recognition through my prayer, but rather a change in you. I want you to have wholeness in your lives, even though you may consider me a great pretender. ⁸ Still, I don't

live in contradiction to reality but in harmony with it. ⁹ I am celebrating my weakness and your strength. I want you to be fully equipped.

¹⁰ I am writing to you my honest feelings in advance of my visit in hopes that you will correct your attitude and behavior. When I arrive with the authority God has given me, I want to be constructive rather than destructive.

¹¹ And now, my fellow Christpersons, here are my final thoughts: be joyful, be mature in your living, encourage yourselves, accept each other's point of view, and appreciate differences. And God who creates love and unity will be manifest in your midst. ¹² Greet each other with an affectionate hug. ¹³ The Godpersons here send their greetings. ¹⁴ May the unconditional love of the Lord Jesus Christ, and the love of God, and the fellowship of the Holy Spirit belong to each of you. Amen!

Galatians

INTRODUCTION

To introduce the book of Galatians is to introduce one of the greatest statements on freedom ever written.

The author is the Apostle Paul, and his original Letter to the Galatians was written not to one congregation, but to the several churches in Galatia. We don't know exactly where all these churches were located, nor when the letter was written, nor where it was written. The consensus is that Paul wrote the letter around 56 or 57 A.D., probably from Corinth. *Galatia* could refer either to a Roman province by that name or to a more ancient geographical area that had been absorbed by Rome.

Fortunately, these particular historical facts are not necessary to understand what Paul was saying in this letter. It is essential that we understand *why* he was writing to the churches in Galatia.

Very simply here is the situation. Paul had heard of some trouble brewing among the Galatian Christians, trouble stirred up by teachers who were called Judaizers. These Judaizers— Jewish-Christian legalists—wanted the Galatian Christians to continue keeping all the Jewish laws, even circumcision.

In other words, one group of Christians (the "insiders," as I have called them, representing the Jewish faction) was trying to convince another group (which I have called the "outsiders," representing the Gentiles) that they could not truly be Christians if they did not obey the rules God gave the Jews.

Paul, of course, was incensed at this step backward into a legalistic trap that negated everything Christ had died for. Thus, his letter to the Galatians passionately proclaimed the superiority of God's free grace over any and all forms of legalism. And not only that—this grace was open to some groups of people who, until Christ came on the scene, were not even considered worthy of notice, much less salvation. People like women—slaves—Gentiles. What a revolutionary notion! No wonder Paul had such a hard time getting through to some of the early Christians. And, I wonder how ready we are to accept this statement of the faith.

There was another side of the issue, though, that Paul also brought to the attention of the Galatians. He wanted them to understand that freedom from rules did not mean freedom from responsibility.

So, freedom and responsibility are the two great overriding themes of Galatians. There are other dramatic stories woven into the letter: Paul's assertion in chapter 1 that the gospel he is preaching came directly from God (he was trying to combat rumors that questioned his authority as an apostle)—and his confrontation with Peter (chapter 2) about Peter's game-playing and hypocrisy. These episodes serve to enhance the fervor which Paul felt about communicating the good news and making sure that those early Christians really understood the meaning of the gospel for their lives.

In my relational paraphrase I have tried to maintain the same kind of passionate excitement with which Paul wrote, because his message in Galatians is just as crucial for twentieth-century Christians as it was for those in the first century.

GALATIANS

1 ¹ I am Paul, God's special messenger to you, not humanly appointed, but installed by Jesus Christ and God the Father who raised him from death. ²⁻³ Both I and all your brothers and sisters here with me send greetings to you in the churches of Galatia, praying that you will experience unconditional love and peace from God and our Lord Jesus Christ. ⁴ Christ unconditionally gave himself for us to overcome our alienation and to enable us by God's will to break the cultural conditioning which has determined our whole life. ⁵ May God receive his own fulfillment in time and beyond.

Be faithful to the good news

⁶ In the face of God's generous act, I am shocked that you have turned away so quickly from the call of God's unconditional love, challenging you to life through Jesus Christ. You have exchanged good news for bad. ⁷ This so-called "good news" to which you have been listening perverts God's true message. ⁸ Damn those persons who are leading you astray! ⁹ I repeat, may those persons who are teaching this perverted message go to hell! ¹⁰ Those who claim I am teaching a freedom style of life for popularity's sake are liars. How can I be doing Christ's work if I am motivated primarily by human approval?

God has called Paul to be a special messenger

¹¹ Let me say it clearly. The good news I have been telling you is not human fantasy. ¹² No human being gave it to me, nor was I taught it; I received this message of God's unconditional love from Jesus Christ himself.

¹³ You have heard about my former lifestyle in the Jewish faith, how I attacked the fellowship of Christpersons—the Church—and tried to destroy it. ¹⁴ I was acquiring a higher reputation than others in the Jewish faith because of my devout dedication to tradition. ¹⁵ But God called me through unconditional love to be his special messenger. ¹⁶ And, in his time he revealed Christ in me so that I might proclaim the good news of his love to those outside my own faith. When I received this special calling, I did not discuss it with a single human being. ¹⁷ I didn't even visit with God's special messengers in Jerusalem, but I went into Arabia and later returned to Damascus.

¹⁸ After three years I went to Jerusalem and visited a couple of weeks with Peter, ¹⁹ but I didn't see any other special messengers except James, our Lord's brother. ²⁰ I am not lying about my unique calling and message, or the way I received both. You have been listening to the liars. ²¹ After I was called and equipped, I went into Syria and Cilicia, ²² before any of the Christians in Judea had ever met me; they only kept hearing that the man who had tried to destroy the Church was now proclaiming God's message of love. ²³ In spite of the fear this news stirred up, these brothers received me and praised God with thanksgiving for what he had done in me. ²⁴ (Why can't you be as generous as they in bringing fulfillment to God through me?)

Paul's relationship with the "higher ups"

2 ¹ I want to tell you a little more about my relationship with the leaders of the Jerusalem church. Not until fourteen years after I met Christ did I go back to Jerusalem and then I took Barnabas and Titus with me. ² I felt an urge to test with them my understanding of the good news which I had been proclaiming to the "outsiders"—non-Jews. So I laid out to all the leaders my grasp of the faith to ensure that my preaching efforts would not be fruitless.

³ Incidentally, some phony Christpersons tried to pressure Titus, an outsider, into being circumcised. ⁴ They slipped into our meeting, and then tried to force us to conform to their rules. ⁵ We did not surrender to them for a minute so that we may continue to tell you Galatian outsiders that you are accepted by God without keeping the "insiders'"—that is, Jewish—rules, circumcision being an example.

⁶ Now, back to my relation with the "higher ups." (Position really doesn't matter with reference to God's acceptance of a person.) These men knew nothing about God's message that I did not already know. ⁷ Instead of discounting my message, they affirmed that I have good news for outsiders as Peter does for insiders. ⁸ You see, they recognized that God was speaking through me to the outsiders just as he does through Peter to the insiders. ⁹ And when James, Peter, and John, the higher ups of the church, realized this, they included us in their fellowship and encouraged us to keep working with outsiders as they did with insiders. ¹⁰ Their only suggestion was to remember the poor—and we were already eager to do that.

Paul confronts Peter's game-playing

¹¹ In setting forth my relation with the leaders in Jerusalem, I must tell you about an incident at Antioch. ¹² There I confronted Peter with his game-playing. Before a delegation came up from Jerusalem, he ate and had fellowship with the outsiders. But when those insiders from Jerusalem arrived, he withdrew and joined them. ¹³ When the other insiders saw his behavior, they joined Peter in withdrawing, and the pressure became so great that even Barnabas joined them. ¹⁴ When I recognized the phoniness of their behavior, I confronted Peter in the presence of the entire community. "Peter," I said, "if you are an insider and yet you live in the freedom of an outsider, why do you pressure these free outsiders to live the constricted lifestyle of an insider?"

Both insiders and outsiders are freed from keeping rules

[15] You know that both insiders and outsiders relate to God the same way. [16] Neither of us has a right relationship with God by keeping the rules. Only by trusting Christ do we experience this relationship, and you can't achieve this relation by keeping rules. Consider this question: [17] If in our eagerness to have this relation with God through Christ we try to obtain it by keeping rules, and then fail, is this Christ's leading? Of course not. [18] If I have given up on rules to provide me a right relation with God and then return to them, I make myself a failure.

[19] Because of what the rules did to me, I have given up on them so that I might have a relation with God. [20] My pseudoself which tried to get a relation with God by keeping the rules has been nailed to Christ's cross; my authentic self has come alive—yet I am not in isolation. I am united with Christ and I keep trusting his love for me, especially as it went into action for me on the cross. [21] I will not nullify God's gift of unconditional love in Christ by returning to a set of rules. If rules could have created a relationship, then Christ's gift of himself is an empty gesture.

A right relation with God comes through trust alone

3 [1] You Christpersons at Galatia have confused me. Who has so clouded your thinking to mix you up about God's love for you? I remember very distinctly how Christ was presented visually to you as crucified. [2] Let me raise a central question to help clear up your thinking. *Did you receive the Spirit by keeping a set of rules or by trusting God to give him to you?* Are you so mixed up in your thinking? [3] If you began this new life by receiving the Spirit as a gift, do you now think

you will mature by keeping rules? [4] Has your experience of God's grace been without significance? Maybe it has. [5] Consider yet another question. When you saw the Spirit miraculously at work in me, was I in bondage to rules? Or did you receive the Spirit through someone free in the Spirit?

[6] Having a right relationship with God through trust alone is not a new idea. Abraham had this right relationship through his trust in God's promise. [7] Now everyone who trusts God is a true descendant of Abraham. [8] Abraham's experience forecasts God's intention to establish a faith relationship with mankind. [9] Now everyone who trusts God has the same fulfillment that Abraham experienced.

[10] In contrast everyone who seeks fulfillment by keeping rules is rejected by God because it is written, "God rejects the person who does not perform perfectly every rule in the rule book." (And you know that's impossible.) [11] It is evident that persons rightly related to God have this relation through trust because "the Godperson lives by trusting God."

[12] The rules are not based on trust, and the person who chooses to live his life by the rules will be imprisoned by them. [13] But Christ has freed us from the condemnation which is the inevitable outcome of trying and failing to keep rules as a way of life. He liberated us by accepting that condemnation for us, and experiencing it on the cross. [14] In so doing he annulled the rules so that the promise of God to Abraham might be received by outsiders, and that we might receive the Spirit by trusting him.

Why and how God gave the rules

[15] Let me use a human analogy. When two parties enter into a contract, neither of them can change it. [16] Now, God made a contract with Abraham and his offspring, and when God said "offspring," he meant Christ. Let me further compare God's contract with a human contract. [17] The contract God made

with Abraham, in which he pledged to relate to all persons through Christ, was not annulled by the rules he later gave. [18] If the bequest had originated in rules, then it would not be a pledge; but God made it as a pledge to Abraham.

[19] You may legitimately ask, "Why did God give the rules?" The rules were given because we did not know how to live a relational style of life until Christ came. They were given through God's messengers with the help of a mediator. [20] In human negotiations a mediator is used for a two-party agreement, but in the case of a pledge, it is a declaration from God's side only.

[21] "Do the rules cancel God's pledge?" you ask. By no means! If a right relationship with God could have come through a set of rules, then we could have done it that way. [22] But the fact is, all of us were estranged from God, and we only have a right relationship with him when we receive it through his pledge in Jesus Christ. [23] Before we learned to trust God's pledge, it was as if the rules imprisoned us and we were locked up until we were shown the way out—the way of trust.

[24] The rules then were like our teacher at school enabling us to discover how much we have gone wrong. They functioned until Christ came to give us a right relationship with God through faith. [25] Through trusting Christ, we have graduated from the classroom of rules. (The analogy is like going from college to life, from training to the actual job.)

[26] I want to be very clear: we are all in God's family through receiving Christ. [27] When you were baptized into Christ, you were given the same relation to the Father that he had. [28] And when you are in God's family, you have an equal standing with everyone else because there is no distinction between races or sexes or social classes. We are all united by Christ. [29] And when you belong to Christ, you are the offspring of Abraham and participate in God's legacy to him.

4 ¹ Here is another comparison: With respect to an inheritance, an heir to a fortune, as long as he is a minor, is no different from a poor person. ² As a child he is cared for by nurses and maids until he comes of age. This illustrates our situation. ³ We have been like children imprisoned in the rules of our culture, ⁴ but at the right time God sent his Son as a human being into a nation governed by rules. ⁵ Why? To free us from the rules and make us members of his family. ⁶ And because you are family members, God has given you the Spirit of Christ so that you can say, "Father, my father." ⁷ You are no longer in poverty, but a child in God's family, and if you are a child of God, then you are his heir through Christ.

Don't slip back into your old ways

⁸ I can understand how, in the absence of a relation with God, you observed empty rites and rituals; ⁹ but now that you have experienced a right relationship with God, it is beyond my comprehension why you would go back to your feeble and ineffective old ways. ¹⁰ You are even religiously observing special days and seasons of the year! ¹¹ Sometimes I feel as though my investment in you neither appreciates nor pays dividends.

¹² My friends, put yourself in my place as I have endeavored to put myself in yours. You have not hurt me. ¹³ You recall that I was having trouble with my eyes when I first proclaimed the good news to you. ¹⁴ You did not make fun of me or reject me because of my poor vision, even though it was a trial to you. Actually, you accepted me as God's messenger, even as Jesus Christ himself. ¹⁵ Now—where is that spirit of generosity? Why, at that time, if it were possible, you would have pulled out your own eyes and given them to me. ¹⁶ Have I become an enemy because I have told you the truth?

¹⁷ Those teachers among you are making a deep impression

on you, but not for your good. They would even exclude you from a relationship with me and demand your total loyalty. [18] It is good to have deep feelings about positive values, not only when I am with you but in my absence as well. [19] My immature children, I am experiencing labor pains for you again until Christ is born anew in your hearts. [20] I do wish I could visit you face to face. Maybe this would help me change my attitude, but as it is, I have lots of questions.

An allegory to help you understand the rules

[21] Tell me one thing, all of you who want to live by rules, do you really understand the rules? [22] Let me try to assist your understanding by using Abraham's two sons as an allegory. One son was born from a slave and the other from a free woman. [23] The son of the slave was born naturally; the son of the free woman was born supernaturally in fulfillment of God's promise to Abraham. [24-26] This allegory represents the two contracts God has made. The slave woman is analogous to Mt. Sinai in Arabia, where the rules which enslave most insiders were given. Mt. Sinai corresponds to the present earthly Jerusalem, the center of Jewish worship. The free woman is analogous to the heavenly Jerusalem, the free world of the Spirit, which is the mother of those who have received freedom through Christ. [27] It reminds me of a scripture: "Celebrate, O barren woman who has never borne a child; break out into cries of joy if you have never been in labor; the deserted wife has more children than the one with a husband."

[28] My friends, just as Isaac was born to Sarah because of God's pledge, we have received new life because of the integrity of God's pledge. [29] But as was true in the past, those who seek their life in keeping rules attack those who receive their life as a gift through the Spirit. [30] To take the allegory a step farther, the scripture says, "Throw out the slave and her son, for the son of a slave will not share

the inheritance of the free woman's son." [31] We are not children of the slave, but of the free woman—so receive your freedom.

Value your freedom and use it wisely

5 [1] My friends, get a firm grip on the freedom Christ has given you and do not let yourself be imprisoned again by rules. [2] If you depend on circumcision (or any performance—like baptism), Christ is of no value to you. [3] If you try to be right with God by keeping rules, you must keep them all. [4] The gift of Christ is canceled when you seek a right relationship with God through rule-keeping; you have rejected God's generous gift in favor of your own performance. [5] But through the Spirit we await with trust the fulfillment of that hope which proceeds from having a right relation with God.

[6] In this new way of relating to God through Jesus Christ, no outward performance or ritual can produce the vital transformation—all that matters is trust in the pledge of God which produces a life of love. [7] You lived in this new reality for a while. I am wondering what got in your way that you no longer live in the freedom that's yours. [8] This shift in your lifestyle did not come from God who calls you to a better way. [9] You know, just one of you reverting to the rules is like a small piece of yeast affecting all the dough. [10] I have confidence in you because your life is centered on Christ that you will not disagree with me. And whoever has been contaminating you with his yeasty instruction will receive the judgment due him.

[11] Those teachers have erroneously told you that I still preach that keeping the rules brings about our right relation to God. If that is so, why am I still persecuted? If I stopped preaching the availability of God's unconditional love through trust alone, I wouldn't offend anybody. The offense caused by the message about Jesus' liberating death would be removed.

[12] Sometimes I find myself wishing that those persons were wiped out who have contaminated your thinking. [13] My brothers and sisters, God called you to freedom, but don't use your

freedom to fulfill your appetites with no regard for others; instead, develop deep, loving relationships with each other. [14] You fulfill all the requirements of the rules when you love each other. [15] If you blame and accuse each other, you will be destroyed rather than built up by each other.

Live in union with the Spirit

[16] Become aware of the spiritual dimension within you and live through the energy of the Holy Spirit. [17] As you live in union with the Spirit, you will not become imprisoned in old, unproductive patterns for getting your needs met. Your old patterns of living fight against the Spirit which is the source of your new life. These two forces are very much a part of you and yet they contradict each other, too, so that you are unable to do what you wish to do. [18] If you live out of the Spirit, you do not have to keep the rules.

[19] Let me illustrate the old patterns to which I am referring: for example, sex outside of marriage, continuous ambivalent feelings, [20] worship of the temporal, trying to manipulate the supernatural, rebellious reactions, childish expressions of your wants, [21] wishing to be somebody else, wiping others out, wiping yourself out with alcohol, drugs, or partying . . . and all your other unproductive patterns. As I told you when I was with you, those who keep living in these old patterns have not gotten in union with the source of life and thus will not enter God's domain.

[22] Those living through God's Spirit are characterized by love, joy, unity, patience, tenderness, caring, trust, [23] true self-esteem, and self-control in all their relationships. Rules can neither create nor deny those qualities in our relationships. [24] Christpersons have renounced their despised self with all its nonproductive patterns of life, no matter how natural they seem. [25] If you really are in union with the Spirit, then live like it! [26] Don't keep yearning for recognition and approval from other people; check out how much you like yourself.

Don't create envy in a brother. Stay away from encounters in which you win while your brother loses. Adopt a plan so both can win.

Living the new life

6 [1] Brothers and sisters, if a member of God's family lapses into old, unproductive patterns of behavior or develops fruitless new ones, you who live out of the Spirit can assist him to recover. [2] While you are helping another in a spirit of gentleness, keep a watchful eye on yourself lest you also get hooked into unproductive patterns. Listen to the cares and concerns of fellow Christpersons and help each other to carry them, in this way fulfilling Christ's rule.

[3] If you have an unrealistic assessment of yourself, you will live a life of illusion. [4] To maintain a balanced estimate of yourself, look at how you function; then you can have confidence in your worth without being dependent upon the approval of other persons. [5] From this standpoint every one of you must assume responsibility for yourself.

[6] Let me share with you some practical advice about living the new life you have discovered. Share both yourself and your possessions with those who have taught you how to live. [7] Don't live under an illusion: God is not inconsistent—his natural laws are dependable. [8] For example, if you cultivate the nonproductive patterns in your life, you will experience emptiness, meaninglessness, and eventually spiritual decay; but if you continue to live in union with the Spirit, not only will you experience real life here and now, you will have life forever. [9] Don't become depressed or discouraged by the anxiety you experience in developing new and positive ways of expressing your being; you will eventually come to maturity if you do not quit the task.

[10] In your relationships, whenever you have the opportunity, choose to do good things for others as well as for yourself;

this suggestion is particularly applicable to members of God's family.

One last appeal

[11] I have personally written this long letter endeavoring to keep you centered in the new way. [12] I want to repeat my evaluation of those teachers who have contaminated your thinking. [13] They want you to participate in their ritual so their leaders will give them approval, and so that they might avoid persecution for taking the cross of Christ seriously. They demand that you keep the rules they themselves don't. Yet when you permit them to impose that way of life on you, they take pride in their manipulative ability.

[14] May God help me to take pride only in what he did for me through Christ on the cross. Through him I am finished with my self-justifying ways of living and I am searching for a style of life consistent with who I really am. [15] In this new style, I say again, external rituals are worthless; all that matters is being the new person you really are. [16] And, all of you, the new "inside" people of God, who live by this basic principle will be in unity with yourselves and with God. [17] I don't want to be approached on this issue again. I choose to manifest the evidence of my faithfulness to Jesus Christ in my life by the way I live and not by an external marking. [18] Friends, may Christ's unconditional love be with your spirit.

Ephesians

INTRODUCTION

The book of Ephesians is one of the richest resources for the Christian in all the New Testament—rich in language, rich in meaning, rich in content. You can read it over and over again, and each time find a new insight into what the Christian life is all about.

Traditionally, the author of Ephesians is said to be Paul, and he probably wrote it about 62 A.D. when he was in prison in Rome. (This was the same period during which he wrote Colossians, Philippians, and Philemon.) Ephesians is not a personal letter in the style of Paul's other correspondence. It is thought to have been a "circular" letter, intended to reach other churches besides the one at Ephesus.

In this letter, Paul wanted to give his readers as complete a concept as possible of the total Christian life—what Christ has done for his people, what their responsibilities are to Christ, and just what it means to be a Christperson.

The new life in Christ is the subject of chapter 2 as Paul explains, "We have all had this style of life at some time—when we followed the irrational and uncoordinated desires of our anxious, estranged nature, all the while feeling guilty and deeply separated from the source of our being. . . . What a difference Christ has made! No longer are you estranged from God, but through Christ's giving of himself on the cross, you have an intimate relation with him."

[121

Paul also stresses the unity of believers (whether "insiders" and "outsiders") and in chapter 3 offers one of his most eloquent of prayers: "I hope you will be able to grasp with all Godpersons the multidimensional love of God—a love broad enough to include everybody, long enough to reach to the ends of the earth, deep enough to unify our human fragmentation, and high enough to reach the very heart of God. Actually, I want you to know the love of Christ which is beyond knowing."

What should life be like in God's family? What about the Christian lifestyle? Chapters 4 and 5 provide models for the searching Christian to look at, and chapter 6 concludes with Paul's wise words about the Christian's "full dress."

I believe that you will discover in Ephesians the answers to many of the questions which are perplexing us Christians today.

EPHESIANS

1 [1] My name is Paul. God appointed me a special messenger of Jesus Christ, and I am addressing you faithful Christpersons at Ephesus. [2] May God's unconditional love and the unity created by our Lord Jesus Christ be with you.

What God has done for you

[3] I can only say "Praise God" for his gifts to us through Christ, who revealed both our possibilities and the power to actualize them. [4] Before God even started to create the world, he picked us out through Christ because he wanted us to live a life of love in the world and become whole persons related to him. [5] Because of his love, God determined to adopt us as children into his family by Jesus Christ. [6] Truly he will be completely fulfilled and praised through the unconditional acceptance he has offered us in Christ.

[7] Through Christ and his death for us, we can be assured that we are delivered from meaninglessness and set again on the track of God's original intention for us. [8] Through this full revelation of himself and his unconditional love in Christ, God has also demonstrated to us how to stay on the track.

[9] God chose his Son to make known the secret which for eons had been hidden deep in his mind, [10] that in time when his purpose has been fulfilled, he will unify all the fragments of his creation in Christ. [11] In this ultimate fulfillment through Christ which God will accomplish as he planned, [12] we who have trusted in God's goodness have a place which he marked off for us from the beginning, which is to bring him ultimate fulfillment.

[13] When you heard the good news that God loves you and accepts you through Christ, you trusted Christ and accepted

[123

God's acceptance of you. [14] As God's pledge to you that you now have a share in the fulfillment of creation, God gave you his Spirit, who will help you achieve this ultimate fulfillment.

A prayer for growing Christians

[15] Because I have heard about your trust in Christ and your love for Godpersons, [16] I continually thank God for you, mentioning you by name in my prayers.

[17] Specifically, I ask God that his Spirit will show you what God is like so that you will really know him—the true God. [18] As the Spirit works in you, I want him to open your mind and imagination, so that you will clearly see what God was planning when he called you to be a Christperson, that you will glimpse how God is enriched through our love and worship of him, [19] and that you will be aware of the incredibly immense strength which is available to us. [20] You see, we have access to resurrection—to the strength and power God demonstrated in Christ when he raised him from death and gave him supreme authority.

[21] Yes, to Christ has been given absolute authority over the whole creation, not only what exists now but also everything which is coming into being. [22] In addition to all of creation, Christ also has full authority over the Church, the fellowship of Christpersons, to give it direction. [23] In the midst of creation, he guides the Church, his body, which fulfills his intention as he fills all things with himself.

Christ gives new life

2 [1] At one time, you remember, you weren't part of this plan. You were dead to God. But God made you come alive to him through Christ. [2] Your former lifestyle was controlled by a set of values inspired by the Adversary who misleads those who have not come alive to God. [3] We have all had this style of life at some time—when we followed the irrational and uncoordinated desires of our anxious, estranged nature,

all the while feeling guilty and deeply separated from the source of our being.

⁴ But we have found God to have extraordinary compassion and immense love for us. ⁵ When we were totally insensitive to him, he cared for us and raised us from death to life through our encounter with Christ. ⁶ To take the analogy of resurrection with Christ further, we ourselves now exercise an authority like that which Christ has in the presence of God. ⁷ God has acted in this fashion to make us recipients of his gracious gift of unconditional love, an example for succeeding generations to behold.

⁸ You have this new relationship with God simply by accepting it. ⁹ It is his gift to you through his unconditional love. It is not something you could ever earn by any effort of your own, so you can't brag about having it, or about doing anything. ¹⁰ No, we are God's artistry, his creative work produced by our relationship to Christ, so that we express the kind of life God originally intended.

Outsiders and insiders in the faith

¹¹ Don't forget, then, that you were "outsiders"—pagans—before you were related to Christ. You were labeled "the uninitiated" by those who had the human initiation of circumcision. ¹² At that point in your life, you were not aware of a relationship with Christ. You were also aliens from the group of "insiders"—the Jews—and their talk of covenants with God sounded strange to you. You had no grounds for hope and no awareness of God in your life.

¹³ What a difference Christ has made! No longer are you estranged from God, but through Christ's giving of himself on the cross, you have an intimate relation with him. ¹⁴⁻¹⁵ Regarding the relation of the outsiders to the insiders, Christ himself created unity between the two by annulling the insiders' rules, laws, and prohibitions—a dividing wall which gave them a distinct advantage. ¹⁶ Having gotten rid of that

unfair advantage, it's now a matter of how each one relates to God. So insiders and outsiders are both related to God in the same way—through Jesus Christ and his death—and there's no room for hostility. ¹⁷ For Christ came to proclaim the unity of all mankind both to those who were near to God and to those who were far away. ¹⁸ Through Christ both sides have come into a close relationship with the Father.

¹⁹ That means you are no longer outsiders or aliens, but on the inside with the insiders; you have a place in the family of God. ²⁰ You are part of his house, which is erected on a secure footing—the special messengers who journeyed with Jesus, and the prophets who told about his coming. ²¹ Jesus Christ himself is the chief stone which causes the whole building to hold together and form a magnificent place for God to live. ²² Each one of you becomes part of it, as Christ creates in you a house in which God lives through the Spirit. (How intimate is our relationship!)

The open secret

3 ¹ Because of the good news about God to you outsiders (who are now insiders), I am in jail for Jesus Christ. ² Possibly you have heard that God through his unconditional love gave me a special call on your behalf. ³ God revealed to me the secret which I wrote about briefly, so now as I elaborate, I hope you will recognize me as one who knows the secret of Christ. ⁴ This secret was not made known in other eras in the way it is now being revealed to God's special messengers by the Spirit.

⁵⁻⁶ The revealed secret is simply that the outsiders are now insiders sharing in the inheritance, the family, and the promises which come from Christ's message of good news about God. ⁷ God gave me the special work of telling the good news in which I am engaged, and it has been enriched by God's unconditional love and his power working in me.

⁸ When I consider God's call upon my life, I am over-

whelmed. I feel less than the least of God's family members when I realize that I have been given the great work of telling you outsiders the full meaning of Christ. [9] And I feel that I must help every person see what this revealed secret means— this secret which has been kept from the beginning of time by God, the creator of all things. [10] But now, in this age God intends even the authorities of the invisible world to know his marvelous wisdom through the agency of the Church, [11] that is, his eternal purpose focused in Jesus Christ before the beginning of time. [12] Through Christ, who is the key to God's eternal purpose, we have a confident audience with the Father through our trust in him.

A prayer for personal growth

[13] I began by telling you about being in jail for your sake, but I don't want my imprisonment to discourage you. It really can add to your fulfillment.

[14-15] Because I don't want you to become discouraged, I offer this prayer to the Father who has given his name to the whole family of God both in heaven and on earth.

[16] May he give you an infusion of strength in the depths of your being by the Spirit. [17] I pray that your trust will enable Christ to settle down in you so that you will be grounded in love. [18] I hope that you will be able to grasp with all God-persons the multidimensional love of God—a love broad enough to include everybody, long enough to reach to the ends of the earth, deep enough to unify our human fragmentation, and high enough to reach the very heart of God. [19] Actually, I want you to know the love of Christ which is beyond knowing. [20] Experiencing love like this, may you be overwhelmed with the awareness of the presence of God.

[21] Now to God, who can do by the power that exists in us greater things than we are able even to imagine or request, to him be the fulfillment he intended through Christ Jesus, now and always. Amen.

On the unity of God's family

4 [1] From this cell where I am the Lord's prisoner, I am urging you to live a life consistent with your adoption into God's family. [2] I trust these suggestions will be helpful. Keep a sane estimate of your capabilities and consider the potential of other Christpersons with a patient, loving attitude. [3] Really try to maintain unity in the family of God; when there is tension, fight fair and do not break with a brother or sister. [4] So many things unite us—the family, the Spirit, [5] the hope, the Lord, the faith, the baptism, [6] and God our Father who transcends all and yet is within all.

[7] Yet we are individuals, and Christ has given each of us gifts, along with divine assistance equal to our gifts. [8] These gifts were given to the members of God's family when the bodily presence of Christ was taken from us. [9] (According to our scriptures, before Christ went away bodily, he went into the heart of the earth. [10] Just as he went into the deepest depths, so also he ascended to the highest heights in order to fill all creation from top to bottom.)

[11] Now a word about the gifts which Christ gives to his family. He first gave the original Twelve who traveled with him. Now he gives agents to sharpen the commitment of the family, witnesses to bring new members into the family, fatherlike leaders to nurture the family, and instructors to teach the family. [12] He acts through these special functions to enable the members of the family to fulfill their mission, which will in turn enrich the entire body of Christ. [13] The ultimate fulfillment of the family of God depends upon each member reaching his full potential as Christ did, yet keeping in unity with the other family members while fully experiencing his individuality.

[14] As we grow toward maturity, we must not be seduced by short cuts, devices created by con men to deter us from serious growth. [15] But as we continue to share honestly with each other, we help one another grow to our full potential as Christpersons

in unity with Christ our head. [16] As each of us stays in union and harmony with Christ, we are energized and consequently give energy to others through Christ, enabling them in their growth and giving love to the family as a whole.

Suggestions to insiders about lifestyle

[17] These suggestions will help you function as an enabler of love in the family: don't slip back into your old lifestyle like those who are still outsiders. These outsiders direct their lives according to the values they concoct in their heads. [18] They don't understand God's intention for their lives, nor the source of their feelings of estrangement. [19] Because of their unawareness, they sometimes get beyond any feeling for the ultimate and dissipate their potential in a totally unproductive lifestyle. What a waste!

[20-21] But as an insider, you are discovering from Christ a different lifestyle through the truth that has been revealed in the humanity of Jesus. [22] He has taught you to discard those unproductive patterns you developed when you did not know your true identity or the source of your being. [23] I urge you to stay closely related to the source of your being, permitting the Spirit to energize your mind. [24] Discover new ways of expressing your new, unique personhood in Christ, ways which are in harmony with who you really are. This new behavior will demonstrate that you have a right relationship with yourself and with God and are becoming a whole person.

[25] Stop playing games, and be straight in your communication, because we are all dependent on each other. [26] Admit your anger when you feel it, but don't be destructive with it. Learn insider ways of handling it promptly. [27] Don't let the Adversary get a foothold, because he can trip you up and you will likely get hooked into some of your old patterns. [28] Don't take what belongs to another. Work hard so that you can provide for yourself and also help those in need. Don't live by short cuts. [29] Don't be destructive in your communication, but let it be in

harmony with who you are. This honest expression of your-self will reveal your values and nurture your hearers, showing them your unconditional acceptance of them. [30] Do not wound the sensitive Spirit of God who is your pledge of ultimate reunion and fulfillment. [31] Negative feelings and practices like hostility, bad temper, anger, creating disturbance, slanderous and malicious gossip are nonproductive in your life. [32] Get rid of them and cultivate kindness, sensitivity, and forgiveness of others, just as you have been forgiven by God in Christ.

More suggestions to insiders

5 [1] Show to others the Father's nature because you are members of his family. [2] Let your life be characterized by the kind of love that Christ had when he offered himself to God in our behalf. Such love will give off a fragrance in your life. [3-4] Because you are Godpersons, avoid practices such as promiscuous sexual relations, sexual perversion, double stand-ards, grasping for more and more. In fact, don't even joke about these things, and avoid meaningless superficial talk. Learn instead to give thanks to God for his good gifts. [5] You are fully aware that persons who commit sexual immorality, or live two lives, or grasp for more and more, or have allegiances other than to God—such people have no family inheritance in God's domain, because they give no evidence of even being in the family. [6] Don't let anyone mislead you: this style of life does not have the approval of God.

[7] So don't get hooked into your old lifestyle. [8] When you were an outsider, you were closed to God's presence, but now you are transparent to him and aware of his presence. Keep on living an open, transparent life, [9] because that is where the Spirit blooms and produces fruit in authentic relationships [10] and demonstrates the kind of life God approves. [11] Again, I urge you not to give yourself to those unproductive ways of living, but show them up for what they are. [12] I am ashamed to describe explicitly the activities of those outsiders. [13] But your

transparency permits God's light to shine on their lives, enabling them to see themselves and discover a new course for their lives.
[14] This admonition is directed toward the outsider, but it applies to us former outsiders as well. God says, "Wake up, you sleepers, open yourselves and Christ will make you transparent, too." [15] Then, as wise persons, keep open to your own depths and to the source of your being. [16] Structure your time productively. [17] Get a clear grasp of God's intention for you. [18] Don't drink wine excessively, but rather drink deeply of the Spirit. [19] When you gather with the Godfamily, learn to celebrate your life together with all kinds of songs. Let your heart sing a melody to the Lord. [20] Cultivate the habit of giving thanks to God through Jesus Christ for everything that happens to you.

Models for family living

[21] Be willing to receive suggestions from each other because Christ may address you through a brother or a sister.
[22] Relationships in your individual family can benefit from the analogy of the family of God. Wives, be responsive to your husbands as Christ's followers respond to him. [23] Men, take responsibility for your families just as Christ does for the Church. You are a provider for your family. [24] As the Church is totally responsive to Christ, you wives should respond to your husbands in every aspect of your relationship. [25] Marriage calls for reciprocal giving, so you husbands must love your wives with the self-giving love that Christ showed for his family, the Church. [26] He gave himself for the Church to purify it. Through reflection upon his Word, [27] the Church, like a bride, purifies herself for a real celebration.
[28] Because of the intimate nature of marriage, a man is really loving himself when he loves his wife. [29] It's unthinkable that a man would hate himself, so when he loves and cares for his wife, he is enriching his own life just as Christ does when he

[131

cares for the Church, [30] which is his body. [31] In the beginning God declared that a man should leave his parents and be united to his wife. [32] In this relationship they should learn to function so that each preserves his or her own personality while responding to the desires of the other. This unity of persons that preserves individuality is a mystery, but that is how it is when we are united to Christ. [33] So you husbands and wives, keep on loving each other and let the miracle keep happening!

6 [1-3] I am continuing to write about how to function in your primary relationships. For example, you youngsters, listen to your parents. Work out your relationship with them, because this is the matrix in which you develop patterns for your relation to Christ. A constructive relationship will serve you well in every other significant relationship of your life. [4] You fathers, I remind you that you have a responsibility to help your children develop a mature relationship with you. Don't always make them angry. Keep in mind that how they relate to you affects how they relate to the Lord.

[5] Those of you who are employees should consider Christ as the real person in power, [6] and respond to him in love rather than destroy yourself with hostility toward your manager or supervisor. [7] Do your task joyfully, knowing that you serve Christ through your vocation. [8] Whatever you achieve, God will reward you whether you are a manager or an employee. (I myself am taking the attitude that I am in this jail for Christ and not my captors.)

[9] If you find yourself in power (an owner or a manager), do not use it destructively on the powerless. Remember that Christ has the ultimate power over both you and them. Learn to share the power together constructively.

The Christian's "full dress"

[10] My brothers and sisters, I have written you a number of directives about living in the family of God. Here is my final

word. Find the source of your strength in the Lord and his power, which is readily available. [11] Like a soldier going out to a battle, put on the armor which God provides so that you may survive in the struggle with the Adversary. [12] Our real struggle is not with other persons, but with those invisible forces which shape life on earth. [13] Because these forces have entrenched themselves in you as well as in others, you will need all the strength you can get to overthrow them.

[14] Get a clear understanding of the truth about God and the truth about yourself and wrap it like a girdle about your hips and thighs. Cover your chest with right relationships, according to the truth you have received. [15] Put on your feet shoes of peace and tread gently through troubled relations. Help every person to win, and struggling will cease. [16] Your confidence in God is your shield, the most important piece of armor you have, and his unconditional love for you will keep you from self-doubt and despair. [17] Wear the reality of your wholeness like a shining helmet on your head, and carry the Word God has spoken like a sword in your hand, with his Spirit in your head and heart. [18] Cultivate a continuous attitude of prayer both for yourself and for the Godfamily.

[19] Remember especially to pray for me that I may have courage to keep telling the mystery of God's love—[20] a story that has at the moment landed me in jail. [21] I know you have been worried about me, and that is why I am sending this letter to you by our beloved brother and trusted fellow worker Tychicus. [22] I want you to know everything, and to be encouraged about me. [23] Peace is yours, my brothers and sisters, and love mixed with confidence from the head of the family— God the Father and his Son, Jesus Christ. [24] May God's unconditional love be with all who take off their masks and state clearly that they love our Lord Jesus Christ.

Philippians

INTRODUCTION

Think of the Book of Philippians as Paul's love letter. In it he speaks warmly and intimately to the congregation at Philippi which he founded and loved so well. Other letters show Paul's theology or his struggles with problem churches, but in Philippians we have a more personal glimpse of Paul the man and of his relationship to these early Christians who were central in his concern.

Paul probably wrote the letter around 61 or 62 A.D. when he was imprisoned in Rome. The church at Philippi had sent Epaphroditus with a gift to Paul, but Epaphroditus became seriously ill, and was forced to stay longer in Rome than he had planned. When he recovered enough to return to Philippi, Paul took the opportunity to write a letter to his beloved Philippian friends, thanking them for their gift, and sharing words of wisdom and counsel with them.

In chapter 1 Paul hastens to assure his readers that even his imprisonment is working toward the glory of God, and he appeals to the Philippian congregation to maintain unity in God's name so that they might spread the good news even more effectively.

The second chapter offers a shining example of what the Christian lifestyle can be, and what Christian relationships involve. Says Paul, "Consider Christ as your model." Chapter 3 continues in this vein, with an added warning to watch out for the "legal-

[135

ists," those who emphasize keeping rules over living a Christ-style life.

The last chapter is highlighted by two points: some "guidelines for your thought life," and the Christian attitude of acceptance—"I have learned to accept my circumstances, whatever they may be."

PHILIPPIANS

1 [1] Paul and Timothy, servants of Christ, are writing this letter to you fellow Christpersons at Philippi and your leaders. [2] May unconditional love be yours as well as the unity of your being which comes from God the Father and our Lord Jesus Christ.

[3] Every time I think of you, gratitude to God fills my heart, [4] and I always pray for all of you with real joy. [5] I am very grateful because you have participated in the spread of the good news from the first day you experienced it until this very day. [6] I am sure that God will continue to expand the new creation he has initiated in you until he completes it on the day when he fulfills all creation through Jesus Christ. [7] Naturally I have this confidence because you have shared so deeply in my life and ministry whether I have been preaching or sitting here in jail. [8] God knows how I long through Christ's mercy to see you again.

[9] Because of our relationship, I ask God to mix more and more love with your intelligence and evaluative power, [10] so that in each situation you will choose the highest good and live without pretense or manipulation until the day of ultimate fulfillment. [11] May you bring to reality all the potential of a right relationship with God through Jesus Christ and thereby fulfill God's intention which magnifies his being.

Paul's reason for being is Christ

[12] My friends, I also want you to know that even my being in jail has helped spread the good news of God's love. [13] You see, even the emperor's guard as well as other onlookers can recognize that I am in prison for Christ's sake. [14] Because many Christpersons witness how I behave under these cir-

cumstances, they have a great deal more courage to share their own witness without fear of the consequences.

[15] I must confess, though, that their witness for Christ springs from contrasting motivation. One group is motivated by jealousy and competition, while another group witnesses out of their deep desire to participate in the ministry. [16-17] Those who witness competitively try to increase my suffering, but the others function out of their own love for God. They know I am committed to my ministry regardless of what anyone else does. [18] But what difference does it make? Whether as a game or as a real ministry, they both are witnessing for Christ and I celebrate the fact that witnessing is going on.

[19] And I will keep on celebrating because I know this attitude will bring my deliverance through your prayers for me and the constant gift of the Spirit from Christ. [20] I don't ever want to be ashamed. Whether I am actually released from prison or not, I expect Christ to radiate through my person by my fearless witness, whether I live or die. [21] My very reason for being is Christ, and dying means more fulfillment for me and for Christ. [22] If I go on living, I will continue my witnessing for Christ. Yet it's hard to choose. I am in a dilemma. [23] To leave this earthly life and be with Christ would mean fulfillment to me personally; [24] yet it is necessary for me to continue in this present mode of existence for your sakes. [25] When I look at my options in this light, I feel confident of my release from jail [26] so that I may help you grow in the faith and celebrate life more fully.

[27] I want you, then, to let your lifestyle commend the good news of Christ to others. Whether I visit with you or get the report verbally, I want to know that you maintain unity. As a united fellowship be diligent in maintaining the cause of Christ. [28] Don't let your adversaries frighten you because they will assume you are phony. The courage you display will also increase your own confidence in God's liberating power, and it will be an omen of your adversaries' defeat. [29] Just remember,

as Christpersons you have been given the privilege of suffering for Christ as well as believing in him. [30] When your pain is as severe as mine, you will face the same dilemma that I do about whether to live or die.

Christ is your model

2 [1] Let me make further suggestions about your lifestyle. Consider Christ as your model. Christ relates to us with encouragement, offering us his community in the Spirit, showing us compassion and forgiveness. [2] Relate to each other as Christ relates to you, and my happiness will be complete. I emphasize—express the love for each other that Christ expresses to you; unite yourselves as firmly as Christ unites himself to you. [3] Don't get your motivation from competition or substitute fulfillments. Have an accurate estimate of yourself and of others, so that you tend to focus on their strengths and on your weaknesses. [4] Be concerned about your brothers' and sisters' fulfillment as well as your own.

[5] Christ's relation to God provides you both the model and the motivation for relating to other persons. [6] Though Christ was equal to God, he did not cling to his prerogative; [7] rather, he divested himself of his divine powers and became a human being, a servant without credentials. [8] And as a human, he relinquished his claim for personal fulfillment and consented to death on a cross. [9] Because he relinquished every claim to meeting his own needs, God fulfilled his being and gave him the supreme place of honor and the supreme name of Lord, [10] so that now, when the name of Jesus is made known, every fragment of creation will bow in submission [11] and acknowledge his name as *Lord* Jesus Christ and his superior fulfilling of the intention of God.

Live like Christpersons

[12] Because of Jesus Christ, my friends, I want you to be obedient to the Father as he was, whether I am present or

absent. Keep discovering your wholeness in him. Take full responsibility for the choices you make. [13] But remember that in all your choices God is at work fulfilling his intention in you. [14] Live your life without complaining and arguing, [15] so that you will be in practice the children of God that you really are—without guilt, hostility, and criticism. Then, in the midst of a nation full of guilt and hostility, you will shine like flood-lights on a dark night. [16] Keep offering your way of life to others so that when you cross the finish line, I can collect on the gamble I have made on you by investing my life in you.

[17] Even if I die in this prison for my faith which I have shared with you, I celebrate in Christ that my life will be mixed with yours. [18] And if I should die, I want you to celebrate my death with me. [19] I am anxious to hear news of you, and I will soon be sending Timothy to visit you. [20] I don't have any other companion who cares so deeply for others as he does. [21] All the others are searching for their individual fulfillment and not the fulfillment of the whole creation that Christ intends. [22] But not so with Timothy. He has worked with me to spread the good news like a son working with his father. [23] I will send him your way when I determine my own condition, [24] and I hope that soon the Lord will let me come to visit you myself.

[25] Since my visit is, however, doubtful, I probably will send Epaphroditus on a return trip. He is a true brother and companion whom you sent to fulfill my needs. [26] He really loves you, and he has felt depressed because you were worried about his illness. [27] Yes, he nearly died, but God was good to both of us by healing him. [28] Because he was so ill, I will send him to you eagerly so that you can have the joy of seeing that he is fine. Your joy will help soothe my own sorrow at not being with you. [29] You may want to plan a celebration to honor him when he arrives. (And don't forget there are others like him.) [30] He is special to the Lord and I hope you will treat him that way. Because, you see, he nearly died fulfilling your ministry

to me—and never once thought of the personal sacrifice he was making.

It's a right relation with God that counts, not rules

3 ¹ In conclusion, my friends, celebrate life in the Lord. I want to repeat what I've already written regarding my values, and it's not a burden to do so because I want you to get settled in your style of life. ² Watch out for persons who bite and devour you with negative remarks and deceptive teaching. Mark those persons whose actions contradict your values. Shun those persons who want to perform external religious rituals on you. ³ Remember, the true ritual begins with a new spirit out of which we worship God through Jesus Christ. We no longer depend on our performance to achieve a relationship with God.

⁴ If we're talking about performance, though, I have more grounds for trusting in my religious performance than those who are confusing you. ⁵ Compare my credentials with theirs. I received the ritual on the proper day. I am an Israelite; my tribe is Benjamin. I am as Jewish as anyone can be. Concerning keeping the rules, I was a Pharisee, and for strictness you cannot top that. ⁶ Concerning zealous activity, I led in the persecution of those who confessed Christ. Concerning keeping the rules, I performed perfectly.

⁷ All these achievements which earned me an enviable place among my peers, I rejected for a relationship with Christ. Furthermore, I reject every human effort to achieve a right relationship with God; I receive it through my experience of Christ. ⁸ I have totally rejected performance as a way to achieve a right relation with God. Consequently, I have lost my standing with my peers—a standing which is repulsive as manure when I compare it to knowing Christ. ⁹ I would rather be in a growing relation with him than be always struggling to get his approval through my own efforts—and I already have this relation with God through trusting Christ.

Paul's goal is the fulfillment of his calling

[10] I want to demonstrate Christ's style of life—to experience the energy of his resurrection, to participate in human suffering, to die, as he did, to my old style of life. [11] And, I hope to experience resurrection from death as he did. [12] This is my desire. And though I have not experienced Christ as completely as I can describe my vision of this life's fulfillment, I keep on pursuing the vision so that I will eventually experience Christ as completely as he has experienced me. [13] But I am under no illusions that I have reached this goal. I have, however, adopted one rule—[14] I turn my back on the past and focus on my one clear objective: the fulfillment of my calling by God through Jesus Christ.

[15] Every mature person should identify this same goal as the central purpose of his or her life. In the process God will help you discover your conflicting motivations. [16] Only be sure you live out whatever level of awareness you have reached—keep in mind that love must determine your choices whatever your stage of growth.

[17] My friends, follow my free style of life and take note of those who live by rules because, [18] as I have already advised you, these legalists are really Christ's enemies. [19] They worship their appetites; they take pride in behavior that would embarrass others; and they are headed for total meaninglessness. [20] In contrast, our lifestyle is conditioned by our ultimate goal, Jesus Christ, [21] who will transform our limited earthly existence into a fulfilled existence like his own, using the same power by which he controls every part of creation.

Work on your thoughts and attitudes

4 [1] My dear and beloved family who are my pride and joy, because you possess the hope I have been writing about, remain firm in your commitment to Christ. In conclusion, I have several admonitions for you. [2] I want Euodia and Syntyche to settle their dispute. [3] Also, I hope that you, my

reliable companion, will assist these women who worked so well with me and Clement and all the others whose names God has recorded, in telling the good news. ⁴ All of you, be joyful! Yes, keep on rejoicing that you belong to the Lord. ⁵ And let everyone see your kind and gracious spirit. For I believe the hour of ultimate fulfillment is near, when our Lord will come.

⁶ Don't be anxious about anything in your life—tell God your needs with a spirit of gratitude. ⁷ And instead of fragmentation you will experience the unity of your being through Jesus Christ. ⁸ Here are some guidelines for your thought life: think reality—worthwhile thoughts, honest thoughts, clear thoughts, loving thoughts, praiseworthy thoughts, whatever has integrity and deserves admiration—these should dominate your thinking. ⁹ Again, I emphasize that if you will keep living the style of life you learned from me, Christ, who demonstrated himself in me and received you, will be with you. God who unifies us with all creation will be with you also.

¹⁰ I am really celebrating in the Lord that now, after such a long time, your concern for me has sprung up again. Not that I believe you ever quit caring; you just lacked the right opportunity and my imprisonment has provided it. ¹¹ I don't mean to give you the impression that my needs have been unmet. I have learned to accept my circumstances, whatever they may be—¹² I can accept put-downs or recognition. In fact I have become thoroughly used to every and all kinds of existence. I can go hungry or be full; I can handle wealth or be poor. ¹³ I can do everything I need to do because Christ is the energizing center of my life. ¹⁴ I don't, however, minimize your contribution to help meet my need.

¹⁵ You will recall that when I first began this mission endeavor, no group but you at Philippi collected money and gave it to me. ¹⁶ When I was in Thessalonica, you sent me a contribution and when my need was serious, you sent a second contribution. ¹⁷ I am not recounting your benevolence because

I want another gift from you, but I do want you to continue to experience the benefit that comes from giving. [18] I really have more than I need because of the recent gift you sent by Epaphroditus. Your spirit of generosity is like a sweet fragrance rising up before God; it really pleases him. [19] Since you have responded to me so generously, let me assure you that out of his wealth God will provide for all your needs through Christ.

[20] To God our Father be the ultimate fulfillment of his purpose throughout all the ages.

Greet every Christperson in your fellowship for me. [21] My companions send their greetings. [22] All the Christpersons here send greetings, especially those in the Caesar's family. [23] May the unconditional love of our Lord Jesus Christ be with each of you.

Colossians

INTRODUCTION

When Paul wrote this letter to the church at Colossae around 61–62 A.D., he was writing to a church founded by someone else, one he had never even visited. Though he was in a Roman jail at the time, Paul was writing to the Colossians about a specific problem of theirs that had come to his attention.

The problem focused on the false teaching that had become quite influential in the church. J. B. Phillips, in his *Letters to Young Churches* (Macmillan, 1958), explains that the false doctrine contained two errors: "First, that the universe contained a number of beings of various degrees of power and importance, ranging from man to God, and that Christ was to be thought of as merely one of the superior powers. . . . The second false tendency was the attempt to force on the Colossian Christians a system of purely arbitrary observances and angel worship, coupled with extreme asceticism. Paul meets this by pointing out the Christian's position in God is far beyond the petty observances of man-made rules. The true asceticism, moreover, is to abstain from evil passions and evil thoughts, not to cut oneself off from the normal use of God's good gifts."

To combat these erroneous beliefs, Paul comes down hard on the absolute supremacy of Christ and his complete adequacy to meet all the needs of our lives. Read verses 14–20 of chapter 1 and notice Paul's fervor as he talks about Christ. In the last part

[145

of chapter 1 Paul points out that the secret of all our relationships is our relationship to Christ.

Paul's strong rebuttal to those who are teaching untruth about Christianity begins in chapter 2. He poses a crucial question: "If you have died to worldly standards with Christ, why do you go on living according to the dictates of culture and tradition?"

Chapter 3 opens with a similar theme: "If indeed you have experienced God's resurrection power, then live a resurrection life!" The rest of chapter 3 and the first part of chapter 4 show what that looks like in daily life.

COLOSSIANS

1 [1] This letter is from Paul, a special messenger of Jesus Christ by God's will, and from our brother Timothy, [2] to our Christian brothers and sisters at Colossae. Greetings through God's unconditional love and the unity he gives through our Lord Jesus Christ.

[3] Timothy and I have thanked God for you in our prayers ever [4] since we heard that you trusted Christ and began to love God's people. [5] We celebrate with you the eternal hope you have through this relation with Christ, a hope you discovered through the good news. [6] The good news of a new relationship with God through Christ is transforming persons everywhere I have been, as it has been transforming you since the very first day you acknowledged God's unconditional love. [7] Epaphras, a much-loved co-worker with Timothy and me, taught you this same truth, and [8] he has been just as faithful in communicating your love to us.

[9] Because of his report we constantly pray for you, asking that you may grasp God's intention for you both in your head and in your heart, [10] so that your lifestyle will please God, your efforts in ministry will be productive, and your understanding of who God is will continually enlarge. [11] We want you to become aware of that vast strength which springs out of your relation with God so that you will have steadiness and be able to endure anything with joy [12] and then you will thank God our Father who makes us adequate through our participation in a community of transparent people. [13] He has released us from the confusion and meaninglessness of a closed life and has opened us up so that we participate in the authority of his Son.

The person and work of Jesus Christ

[14] Let me expound on who this Son is and what it means to participate in his authority. Through him we have been restored to God's original intention; our refusal to obey God has been forgiven. [15] Christ is the visible, human expression of the invisible God; he is the first son through whom God wills to have many sons. [16] By his agency all creation came into being, I mean everything in the universe, both the seen and the unseen, every power, force, rule—everything was made by him and for him. [17] Christ is prior to all creation and through him all creation holds together. [18] He is also the Church's head —the whole fellowship of Christpersons is his body. He is the first example of real life through his victory over death, a victory which gives him authority over all creation. [19] By God's choice he expresses completely what is divine. [20] Through Christ's self-giving act upon the cross, God has united himself to all people and all creation; and I do mean everything, whether human beings and the created world or heavenly beings.

[21] You yourselves were estranged from God; you were at war with God's intention both in your thoughts and actions, [22] but he has restored persons like you through Christ's self-giving act. He intends for you to be complete, guiltless, and free of negative judgment in your relation to him. [23] To fully experience this restoration, you must continue in the faith with resolute determination. Do not veer away from the hope sparked in you by the good news which has been proclaimed to every person and of which I am a messenger.

Paul's special task

[24] I am happy to have experienced pain on your behalf. In so doing I am sharing Christ's sufferings at the present moment for the sake of his body, the Church. [25] You must remember that I am a special messenger, given the special task of bring-

ing to fulfillment God's intention for you, [26] which has been a secret concealed all these years. But now it is openly shown to God's people. [27] God also wills for you outsiders to know the wealth of his own fulfillment through your addition to his family. The secret to which I refer is Christ's intimate relation to you now—the hope of ultimate fulfillment. [28] So I continue to proclaim Christ to every person, warning and teaching everyone, because I want to enable each one to be mature in relation to Christ. [29] That's why I keep working so hard at the task, pushed on by God's action on me.

Focus on Christ; beware of being sidetracked

2 [1] I want to communicate clearly the depth of my concern for you and the brothers and sisters at Laodicea and for all those I have never met face to face. [2] I want each of you to be more at home with yourself, to have unity in love, to experience fulfillment through a growing confidence and understanding and to affirm the secret God revealed through Christ. [3] Christ is the key that unlocks the treasure chest of God's wise purpose and plan.

[4] I want to offer you guidance in living your faith so that no so-called spiritual leader will seduce you with his appealing language. [5] I may be physically absent from you, but I am present in spirit, overjoyed to see your self-discipline and determination as Christ's followers. [6] Keep on building your style of life on the relationship you have with Christ. On this foundation, stack the brick and mortar of your daily choices. [7] And, as I taught you, sing and shout and celebrate as you lay one brick on another.

[8] Be on the lookout for confusing teachers with deceptive ideas which originate in human traditions and legalistic religion and not in God's revelation in Christ. [9] Focus your attention on Christ, whose life fully reveals the nature of God, [10] and you will find fulfillment through your relation to him,

for he has authority over all earthly powers. [11] Through God's Spirit, Christ has administered in your inner being a sacred rite much like the external rite of circumcision which the Jewish people administer to their children. [12] Or, consider another way of expressing this relationship. It's like being buried with Christ in death by the act of baptism, and then being raised from death with him through your trust in God's action.

[13] In the past you were totally unaware of God because of your repeated refusal of his relationship, and you were entrenched in your rejection. Yet God has made you sensitive to his presence through Christ and on account of him has overlooked your constant refusals. [14] By the cross, God has wiped out the rules which actually blocked our becoming what God intended. He has completely abolished that way of life by nailing it to the cross. [15] And by his resurrection, Christ demonstrated the emptiness of every earthly power when God acts. You have this kind of triumph in life because of your relation to God through Christ.

You are free from worldly standards

[16] Don't let anyone criticize you for what you do or don't eat or drink, or for whether or not you observe certain days, certain times of the month, or the sabbath. [17] These traditions are merely shadows, but Christ has now revealed the reality.

[18] Don't let anyone persuade you that the fulfillment which you have through a vital relation to Christ can be improved by punishing your body or devoting your attention to the worship of angels and demons. Those who promote these practices are trying to penetrate an area of knowledge that is closed to them. [19] They are not holding firmly to Christ. As the head of the body, Christ nourishes every part so that it is united and works together with every other part, and the whole body develops with God's supply of himself. [20-21] Now, let me pose this crucial question. If you have died to worldly standards with Christ, why do you go on living according to the

dictates of culture and tradition? All those commands not to touch, taste, or handle don't apply to you any longer, [22] because they deal with perishable stuff and transient human values. [23] These ascetic practices may get attention for you, but they don't improve your relation to Christ at all.

New patterns of behavior for Christpersons

3 [1] If indeed you have experienced God's resurrection power, then live a resurrection life. [2] Focus your attention on values that endure, not on things which quickly pass away. [3] In a sense you have already passed away, and your life is already firmly united with Christ in God. [4] When Christ, the source of our life, appears, we will then experience ultimate fulfillment.

[5] Here are the implications of having died with Christ: have no sexual expression outside of marriage; don't give undisciplined expression to every passionate feeling, and don't keep grasping for more and more—that is, making a god out of desire. [6] This behavior identifies those outside the family who are estranged from God. [7] Your own lifestyle was once built on your physical passions when you lived according to their dictates.

[8] Lay aside those patterns of behavior, and eliminate the more subtle expressions of your former lifestyle: destructive feelings toward yourself and others, and disrespectful or vulgar conversation. [9] Don't play games with each other—you have pulled off your mask [10] and are now expressing your new self which has been restored to an awareness of God's original intention. [11] This new self knows no distinction in persons. It does not differentiate between special nationalities, between those who practice special rituals and those who do not, between the cultured or the uncultured, the privileged or the underprivileged, the majority or the minority. No, Christ is the ultimate fulfillment for all of these and belongs to every one of them.

[151

Suggestions for enriching relationships

[12] My friends whom I love deeply, dress your new self with the appropriate new clothes—those which enable you to relate constructively to each other. Out of your new self express a generous attitude, kindness, a proper estimate of yourself, tenderness, patience, [13] and especially humility, so that when you have differences of opinion, you can look at the problem from the other person's viewpoint. After a heated argument forgive each other's offensiveness just as Christ forgave you. [14] As the most important piece of new clothing, be sure to wear love, because love is the evidence of maturity. [15] Let unity with God keep watch in your heart, and by all means listen when it warns you of approaching dangers. And, learn to be grateful. [16] Always be aware of Christ in your worshiping community, and with hearts brimming over with the love of God teach and encourage each other with scripture, hymns, and songs of praise. [17] Let your whole style of life, words and deeds, portray your relationship to Christ and be a living expression of gratitude to God.

[18] I have made suggestions to you that will enrich relationships in the family of God; now let me offer suggestions for your individual families. Wives, when you are renewed inwardly, be sensitive to your husbands' needs and wants. [19] Husbands, give your wives unconditional love and do not collect resentments against them. [20] Children, respect your parents and be responsive to their guidance because this pleases the Lord. [21] Fathers, do not wipe out your children's self-confidence, causing them to feel helpless and worthless. [22] Employees, do whatever your employer asks, not just to serve and please him, but to serve and please God as well. [23] In fact, everything you do should be done with enthusiasm because you are doing it for the Lord and not for men. [24] Remember, your pay-off comes in your inheritance from Christ because you serve him. [25] If you create broken, destructive

relationships, you will receive the pay-off for that, too—and it makes no difference who you are.

4 [1] Employers, be fair in dealing with your employees, remembering your own employer in heaven. [2] Keep an open line of communication to God with a grateful attitude and be responsive to what he says. [3] Mention me to God so that he will give me further opportunity to share with others the secret of Christ for which I am now in prison. [4] I want to tell God's secret with all possible clarity and potency. [5] In your lifestyle, act intelligently toward outsiders to the faith, and make good use of your time with them. [6] Learn to converse about things that really matter, things with depth. Especially learn to articulate clearly to every type of person the meaning of your life.

Concluding greetings

[7] Tychicus, my brother and dependable fellow worker, will tell you how things are going with me. [8] I am sending him to you to learn about your condition as well. [9] I am also sending with him Onesimus, who is from your community. They will give you a full report on my situation. [10] My fellow prisoners Aristarchus, Mark who is a cousin of Barnabas (you've already heard about Barnabas and if he comes, welcome him) [11] and Jesus Justus send their love and best wishes. These are the only Jews who have been helping me in working for God, and they have been a source of strength to me. [12] Epaphras, one of your own, a servant of Christ, sends you a special greeting and he prays for you constantly that you may attain spiritual maturity and a sense of assurance. [13] I see what a great concern he has for you and for all the Christians in nearby communities. [14] Luke and Demas also send greetings. [15] Give our love to the brothers and sisters in Laodicea, and to Nympha and to the church which meets in her house. [16] After you have read this letter, exchange it for

the one I wrote to the Christpersons at Laodicea. [17] Oh yes, remind Archippus to be diligent in fulfilling the calling upon his life.

[18] *I am personally inscribing this final word—remember my imprisonment. God's unconditional love be with you.*

First Thessalonians

INTRODUCTION

This is Paul's first letter to the church in Thessalonica, Greece, and it is the oldest of the New Testament writings, having been written around 50 or 51 A.D.

Why was Paul writing to the Thessalonians? Paul, Timothy, and Silas had come to Thessalonica from Philippi, and had established a church there whose membership consisted almost entirely of Gentile converts. Because of bitter persecution (primarily from the Jews in Thessalonica), the three men fled to Berea, about fifty miles away, but the Thessalonian troublemakers followed them and caused so much trouble that Paul had to leave and go on to Athens. When Timothy joined him later in Athens, Paul sent him back to Thessalonica because he was worried about the young, immature congregation there. Paul had not been able to be with them long enough to insure the stability of their faith and answer all their questions.

When Timothy returned from Thessalonica, he joined Paul in Corinth and told him how the new church was faring and what some of its problems were. Paul, in turn, then wrote this "first letter to the Thessalonians." (See Acts 16–17.)

What did Paul write about? 1 Thessalonians may be divided into two parts. Chapters 1, 2, and 3 deal with personal matters concerning Paul and his past work in Thessalonica. Chapters 4 and 5 deal with doctrinal and practical matters in the little group. In particular, the Thessalonians were confused about

First Thessalonians

Paul's teaching on the second coming of Christ, and he goes to some lengths to enlighten them and allay their fears. (This book is noted for its emphasis on eschatology—the doctrine of the end.)

Paul's first letter to the Thessalonians is valuable not only from a historical viewpoint in giving us a glimpse into the very early life of the church, but also from a doctrinal viewpoint, in its cogent presentation of the end times.

FIRST THESSALONIANS

1 ¹ I, Paul, along with Silas and Timothy, warmly greet you brothers and sisters in the Thessalonian church who have a personal relation with God and the Lord Jesus Christ. May you experience unconditional love and peace.

Modeling the Christ-style life

² In our prayers we always give thanks to God for all of you. ³ We constantly recall the practical ways you demonstrate your faith, love, and patient hope, qualities which were inspired in you through your relation to Christ; and God is aware of your behavior. ⁴ Furthermore, we are confident, beloved friends, that God selected you ⁵ because when I spoke the good news to you, I didn't use empty words—my words were potent, inspired by the Holy Spirit, full of confidence, and modeled by my life. My message and my person were one and the same.

⁶ I recall that you began to model your lives after mine as I modeled mine after the Lord. At times your commitment has incurred suffering for you, but you have a source of joy in the Holy Spirit. ⁷ You yourselves have now become models for those Christians in your immediate vicinity and beyond. ⁸ I say "beyond" because your witness has spread far and wide so that everywhere I go I hear about you—I don't even have to bring the subject up. ⁹ The witness I hear from those you have affected has the same clarity and potency that my own witness had to you. This clear reproduction of my model assures me of the effectiveness of my work, because you turned away from physical representations of God to the real, living God, choosing to live intentionally ¹⁰ and to wait expectantly for the fulfillment of life through God's Son, whom he raised

[157

from death and through whom he delivered us from ultimate meaninglessness.

Paul's ministry among the Thessalonians

2 [1] My brothers and sisters, you know that my visit to you was not useless. [2] Even though I had experienced severe physical and emotional pain before arriving in Thessalonica, yet in God's strength I courageously spoke his good news to you amid a great deal of conflict. [3] But in persuading you to believe the good news, I was not deceptive, nor manipulative, nor game-playing. [4] God trusted me with the good news and I have faithfully passed it on, not primarily for your or any person's approval but to please God, who examines our inner selves. [5] I boast quite openly that at no time did I try to con you or control your choice; [6] neither did I seek my greatest fulfillment from any human person, not from you or anyone. That burdensome demand, which I might have made as special representative of Christ, would be too heavy to lay on any person.

[7] Rather than burdening you, I was tender in my relationships with you, like a nurse taking care of children. [8] I loved you so much that I would have given you my life as well as the good news of God's love. Truly you were that dear to me. [9] You do recall how hard I worked at my craft so that I could pay my own way without troubling you. I worked day and night because that was the only way I could tell you God's good news without requiring material assistance from you. [10] You witnessed my behavior, as did God—I was completely absorbed in God's will, full of integrity and beyond criticism. [11] You remember how I encouraged you, guided you, and challenged you, just like a father does his children, [12] to adopt a style of life that will reflect the standards of God who has invited you into his family for the fulfillment of his purpose.

[13] I am constantly grateful to God because you received my communication not as a mere human communication but as

it truly is—the communication of God himself that effects a dynamic activity in you believers. [14] The result has been that, like Christ's followers in the Judean churches, you too have experienced rejection and abuse. [15] The Jews who abuse them and persecute you were responsible for the crucifixion of Jesus our Lord; they even killed their own prophets and expelled us. Their behavior displeases God and harms persons in so far as [16] they forbid us to proclaim the good news to the non-Jews and invite them into a right relationship with God. The Jews want them separated from God completely. Believe me, God totally rejects their behavior.

[17] My friends, I have been away from you physically for a short time, but in my heart I have been by your side through all the pain you've experienced. I have wanted so much and have really tried to get back to see you personally. [18] I would have had a return visit to you by now, but the Adversary blocked the way. [19] Because you know the source of my hope and my joy and my ultimate grounds for feeling successful when Christ comes, don't you? [20] *You* are! You are my fulfillment and joy.

3 [1] When I could no longer endure the anxiety I felt after I left you, [2] I decided to remain in Athens while I sent my brother Timothy—my partner in God's work—to teach you clearly and to encourage you in your faith. [3] I don't want anyone to turn away from Christ because of the pain which you suffer through rejection and abuse; suffering may be our lot. [4] When I was with you, I told you that you would likely experience abuse and you certainly have. [5] Because of my anxiety over how you were handling your suffering, I needed a direct report on you, in case the Adversary made you leave your new life and all my efforts had come to nothing.

[6] But now having received such a positive report on your faith and love from Timothy, plus the fact that you recall my work with appreciation and really want to see me, [7] my anxiety and distress regarding your commitment have been eased. [8] I

can face the future with strong confidence if you are sticking to your commitment to the Lord. [9] How can I express my gratitude to God for all the joy I feel about you? [10] I keep on praying all the time, because I really want to see you face to face so that I may enable you to bring your faith to completion.

[11] So may God, who is our Father, and our Lord Jesus, open the way for me to come to you. [12] And may the Lord teach you the meaning of love and how to express it to each other as I express love to you. [13] I want you to learn to love so that you may be secure before God in wholeness and without any blame when our Lord Jesus Christ appears with all the other members of the family.

Growing in the Christ-style life

4 [1] Also, my brothers and sisters, I urge you to keep on growing in the style of life I described to you when I was there with you. Live like that and you will fulfill God's purpose as well as truly fulfilling your own destiny. [2] You recall the directives which we gave you in behalf of the Lord Jesus. [3] God wills that you be completely united with the purpose of your life, your destiny; and, of course, this means avoiding sexual immorality.

[4] Let your relation to your wife, especially regarding sex, be directed by your new values. [5] You must not surrender to every sexual desire like the outsiders who don't know God. [6] Do not break the moral rules and wrong another person in this area, because God is judge and upholds the rules. [7] You see, God has not called us into a life of perversion or fragmentation but to fulfillment. [8] Anyone who rejects this fulfillment is not rejecting a man like me, but God himself who makes us aware of his Spirit in us.

[9] With regard to loving each other, you do not need me or anyone to repeat my instructions because God himself has taught you to love one another. [10] And truly you are loving all

the family of God in the surrounding countryside, and I urge you to keep on loving more and more. [11] Also, discover ways to lead a peaceful life, to mind your own business, and to do some manual work so that you keep in touch with God's creation. [12] Living in this fashion will win you respect from outsiders and free you from dependence on others.

About those who have died

[13] Now let me give you some information concerning those persons who have died, so that you won't grieve like people who have no hope beyond this life. [14] We believe that Jesus died and arose from death, and that through him God will bring to life all those persons who have died. [15] God instructs me to say that none of us who are alive at the climax of history will have priority over those who have died. [16] At that moment of ultimate fulfillment the Lord himself will appear with the declaration of victory, with the full accord of heaven, and the authority of God himself, and those who have already died will experience resurrection. [17] Then, all of us who live until that hour will be joined to the Lord in resurrection for this family reunion. After the celebration we will be with him always. [18] Encourage and comfort each other with these words of assurance.

Be ready for Christ's return

5 [1] My Christian friends, you do not need me to set dates or mark periods for Christ's return. [2] You are fully aware the day will come as unexpectedly and unpredictably as a robber. [3] When the world around you is proclaiming peace and security, the break-in will occur as suddenly and unannounced as labor comes on a pregnant woman, and it will be as irresistible.

[4] As members of God's family, however, you are no longer blinded by the darkness, so that the day will not creep up on you as a robber. [5] You are children of the God of light, and

[161

you live your lives in open daylight. None of us hides our true identity or lives blindly. [6] No, we must be aware of the meaning of daily events as well as become sensitive to our own feelings, to the presence of God, and to other members of the family.

[7] Those who are unaware are like people who are fast asleep or like drunken persons staggering down unfamiliar streets. [8] But let those of us who are aware be serious about life, protecting ourselves with a growing trust in God and his unconditional love, and a persistent expectation of ultimate fulfillment. [9] For God does not intend our destruction; rather, he intends that we receive personal fulfillment through our Lord Jesus Christ. [10] Christ gave himself for us so that whether we are still alive when he returns, or whether we have already experienced physical death, ultimately we will live with him. [11] Because of this hope, keep on encouraging and strengthening one another, just as you are already doing.

Some final words of advice

[12] I urge you to provide materially for those who are doing God's work in guiding and counseling you. [13] Also, hold them in high esteem and love them for their efforts in ministry. Keep unity among yourselves.

[14] Finally, brothers and sisters, I have a number of admonitions for you. Warn the idle; console the discouraged; sustain the weak; be patient toward all.

[15] Don't try to resolve conflicts by dirty fighting, but find constructive solutions good for everyone—both inside the family of God and outside it.

[16] Keep the spirit of rejoicing.

[17] Make your life a prayer.

[18] Be grateful in each experience of life because God in Christ wants you to have a positive attitude toward life.

[19] Don't try to stifle the Spirit of God.

[20] Recognize the gift of witnesses, but don't be gullible. Prove their statements and keep what is good for you.

[21] If anything appears to contradict God's intention for your life, don't involve yourself with it.

[22] Avoid questionable behavior.

[23] As you adhere to these admonitions, God himself will enable you to be completely in harmony with his intention for you, and will keep you whole and sound in every part—spiritually, emotionally, physically—until our Lord Jesus Christ returns. [24] This is what God wants for you, and you can count on him to make it happen.

[25] Pray for us, my friends.

[26] Embrace each other warmly.

[27] Please be sure to have this letter read to all the brothers and sisters.

[28] May the unconditional love of Christ be with you. Amen.

Second Thessalonians

INTRODUCTION

Traditionally, the second letter to the Thessalonians is thought to have been written by Paul from Corinth, probably around 51 A.D. (or at least shortly after his first letter to the young church at Thessalonica). Though a number of respected critics and theologians question the authenticity of Pauline authorship for 2 Thessalonians, I will hold to the traditionally accepted view.

The reason Paul wrote a second letter so soon after the first is that he had not been completely effective in communicating what he wanted to say about the Second Coming of Christ. Apparently some members of the church were still unclear about Christ's coming "day of conquest"; they still insisted on believing that the end was so near that there was no need for them to work, a practice which did not reflect well on the early church.

A key passage in the book is 2:1-12 in which Paul elaborates again on what the end times will be like. It is not an easy passage to understand, but it bears scrutiny because of its significance.

Chapter 3 contains Paul's exhortation to the Thessalonian Christpersons to take responsibility for themselves. He considers it unforgivable that some persons, in the name of Christ, are actually loafing and trying to get others to take care of them. The theme of responsibility is important, and will be echoed again in later writings of Paul.

SECOND THESSALONIANS

1 [1] My name is Paul, and with the assistance of Silas and Timothy I am dictating this letter to the Thessalonian congregation which has its source in God our Father and direction through the Lord Jesus Christ. [2] May you have unconditional love and the unity of your being through God our Father and the Lord Jesus Christ.

The day of justice is coming

[3] We are obliged to thank God for you because you are growing so rapidly in your trust relation with God and in the abundance of love which you have for each other. [4] In every church we visit, we brag on the way you have patiently endured persecution and pain while keeping your trust strong. [5] Your endurance is evidence of God's justice. Indeed, you will not go unrecognized in his domain.

[6] I believe God will punish those persons who harass you, [7] and will give rest to those of you who are being harassed, as well as to us. Our time is coming when the Lord Jesus will reappear from heaven with his reinforcements. [8] In that day the justice of God will be clearly expressed through him to those persons who have refused to acknowledge God's purpose for their lives and have rejected the good news which he previously brought. [9] These persons will receive what they have chosen—banishment from God's presence and from participation in the ultimate fulfillment of his being. [10] This final day will come when our Lord is fulfilled by the persons who have received him and marveled at by those who have trusted him. You will share in the fulfillment because you believed my witness about Christ.

[11] We pray that God will enable you to have a style of life

that expresses this new reality to which he has called you. May he bring to fulfillment all your good intentions and every act inspired by faith ¹² so that Jesus Christ will be fulfilled and you along with him. This fulfillment originates in the unconditional love of God expressed in Jesus Christ our Lord.

The ultimate contradiction of man

2 ¹ Because one day our Lord is coming to conquer his Adversary and because we are going to gather to meet him, I urge you ² not to be shaken in your mind and not to be in a stew. Nor should you let letters from impostors distress you when they suggest that Christ's day of conquest has already come. ³ Don't permit anyone to confuse you, because that day of triumph will not come until the ultimate expression of evil first appears; he will be the ultimate contradiction of what God intended man to become, ⁴ and will set himself against everything which we hold sacred. This man who totally contradicts God's intention will present himself as God and endeavor to get persons to worship him.

⁵ Recall how I painted this picture when I was with you? ⁶ You are aware that God's Spirit resists the actualization of this contradictory man at the moment. ⁷ Already the forces of evil are seeking to create such a man, but the Spirit resists his appearance and will continue to do so until he is removed. ⁸ When the Spirit's resistance ceases, this ultimate expression of evil will appear, but Jesus our Lord will conquer him by his irresistible authority and the authenticity of his being. ⁹ This contradictory man who expresses the will of the Adversary will have tremendous power to deceive and manipulate ¹⁰ those persons who are increasingly insensitive to the Spirit of God because they refused to believe the truth and become whole. ¹¹ God will permit them to delude themselves and to be convinced by lies. ¹² This will result in utter loss for those who live for temporary pleasure and who refuse to believe the truth and choose to follow the ultimate contradiction

of man instead of Christ, who is the ultimate expression of man.

You have been chosen for wholeness

[13] I must show my deep gratitude to God for you, my brothers and sisters who are loved by the Lord. God has chosen you for wholeness; through the truth I proclaimed to you, he has set you apart by the Spirit's action upon you. [14] By the good news I preached, he has called you to find your fulfillment in our Lord Jesus Christ.

[15] Since this is true, my friends, hold steady and keep the traditions you have received from me, both through letters and my personal word to you.

[16] May Jesus Christ who directs our lives, and God who gives us unfailing encouragement and bright expectations through his unconditional love, continue to encourage you as your new behavior becomes natural.

3 [1] I have a final request, my friends. Pray for us that God's word may be communicated effectively through us and be fulfilled through our efforts just as you are fulfilled by him in what you do. [2] Also, pray that we will be able to avoid irrational and evil persons, because not every person believes.

[3] I remind you that you can count on God to help you build constructive patterns of behavior and to protect you from the unproductive patterns that have controlled your lives. [4] God does give me confidence in your loyalty—that you are doing what I taught you and that you will continue to. [5] May the Lord guide you to recognize his love and to patiently expect Christ to appear.

Take responsibility for yourselves

[6] I want you to keep one rule which I made for you. Do not associate with a brother or a sister who is living without discipline and not like a Christperson. [7] Imitate the behavior which I modeled before you. You recall how I disciplined myself. [8] I

[169

didn't sponge off you, but personally worked hard day and night to provide both my food and lodging so that I didn't cost you a cent. ⁹ I didn't refuse your assistance because I had no right to it, but because I wanted to provide you a good example of Christian ministry. ¹⁰ You recall when I was with you I stated, "Every person is responsible for taking care of himself." ¹¹ I keep getting rumors that members of your group try to make others responsible for them while they loaf and gab. ¹² (If any of you irresponsible persons reads this letter, in the name of Christ, go to work and take care of your own needs.)

¹³ My friends, don't get tired of doing the right thing. ¹⁴ If any reject what I have written about taking responsibility for themselves, mark them and put them to shame by not including them in your fellowship. ¹⁵ I suppose that sounds like asking you to punish them, but I only want you to help them, as a brother or sister, to change their attitude and behavior.

¹⁶ May the one who unites all things, unite you with yourself and with those to whom you relate in everything. May the Lord always be present to you in every experience of life.

¹⁷ This final word is written by my own hand, a mark which identifies all my letters. ¹⁸ May the unconditional love of our Lord Jesus Christ be with all of you. Amen.

Philemon

INTRODUCTION

This letter of Paul is one of the shortest books in the New Testament and one with a very specific purpose. It was written probably about 62 A.D. while Paul was in prison in Rome, to Philemon, a wealthy member of the church at Colossae concerning Philemon's runaway slave Onesimus. Under Paul's influence, Onesimus has become a Christian in Rome and must return to his master (who is also thought to have been a convert of Paul).

Paul has become very attached to Onesimus, and in his letter appeals to Philemon to receive Onesimus with "tenderness and forgiveness." Paul also points out how valuable Onesimus has become, not in terms of his monetary value as a slave, but in his work as "one committed to the good news."

It is significant that Paul makes no statement in this letter about the rightness or wrongness of slavery as an institution. One explanation is that Paul saw no pressing need for social reforms such as the abolition of slavery, since he was convinced that the present world was rapidly coming to an end and that the primary energy of Christpersons should be spent on spreading the good news as vigorously as possible.

PHILEMON

1 [1] I am Paul, in jail for Jesus Christ. My companion Timothy and I write to you, Philemon, our much loved fellow worker. [2] We include Apphia whom we love, Archippus who has been drafted with us into the service of the Lord, and the entire Christian fellowship which meets in your house. [3] May unconditional love and union with God be yours from our Father and from the Lord Jesus Christ.

[4] When I pray, I speak your name to God with thanks [5] because I have heard of the love and trust which you have in the Lord and toward all Godpersons. [6] I pray that your fellowship with me and Timothy in our common faith may give you a deeper understanding of all the possibilities that our union with Christ brings. [7] You must know, my brother, that I am greatly encouraged by your love because numerous Godpersons have been refreshed through you.

[8] Because of my relation to Christ, I could act authoritatively in the request I am about to make [9] but I choose to make my request in a spirit of love, as an old man in jail for Jesus. [10] I am making a request for Onesimus, my spiritual son whom I have fathered while in jail. [11] I realize that in the past he was of little value to you, but with this change in his life he is valuable to me and I believe he will be to you also. [12] Because of this conviction, I have sent him back to you. Receive him with tenderness and forgiveness as though he were a part of me. [13] I would like to have kept him here with me so that in your place he could minister to me in prison as one committed to the good news. [14] Without consulting with you, however, I chose not to keep him here, because I do not want this special benefit without your free approval. [15] He left you for a time like the prodigal son. I hope you as a merciful father will re-

ceive him forever. [16] Receive him now not as a slave but as a dear brother, dear to me and more dear to you as a person and as a Christperson.

[17] If you consider me a partner with you in the faith, receive him as you would me. [18] If he has wronged you, if he owes you anything, charge that to me. [19] Here is my signature to guarantee payment.   PAUL.   I do not want to remind you, Philemon, that all of you owe me your very lives. [20] Dear brother, relieve my anxiety, release my joy because we are Christpersons together. I need your encouragement in the Lord.

[21] Because of my great confidence in your doing what I have asked, I have written this request. Of course, I believe you will be more generous than I have asked. [22] I also make another request of you. Prepare a room for me, because I hope to be released from jail through your prayers.

[23] Epaphras, my fellow prisoner for Christ, sends his greeting [24] along with Mark, Aristarchus, Demas, Luke, my fellow workers. [25] The unconditional love of our Lord Jesus Christ be with your spirit.